Out from the Shadow of Other Gods II

Starting Over

SECOND EDITION

By

Gordon C. Brownlee

with

Linda Haarstad

All scripture quotations, unless otherwise indicated, are taken from the HOLY BIBLE, NEW INTERNATIONAL VERSION®. NIV®. Copyright ©1973, 1978, 1984 by International Bible Society. Used by permission of Zondervan. All rights reserved.

Out from the Shadow of Other Gods II
© 2004, 2015 By Gordon C. Brownlee
Published by Shadow Free Press
Longview, Washington 98632

All rights reserved. No part of this publication may be reproduced or transmitted in any form or by any means without written permission of the author. Copyright 2004, 2015

Out from the Shadow of Other Gods: Starting Over / Gordon C. Brownlee with Linda Haarstad

ISBN 0-9754475-4-8

Notice: The information in this book is true and complete to the best of our knowledge. It is offered with no guarantees on the part of the author or Shadow Free Press. The author, publisher and affiliates disclaim all liability in connection with the use of this book.

**Dedicated to
Brandon and Brett with love and affection.**

**That you might know a Gospel that is free
of the "tree" and the religion of "me."**

Acknowledgments

This book would have not been possible without the help of a number of talented people. Among those deserving special thanks is Linda Haarstad, who spent countless hours deliberating with me about the Gospel and even liked it. She also spent much time formatting, editing and reediting these pages because it was her assignment from heaven. Quite frankly, she made me sound real good!

With love and a very warm thanks to Dona M. Brownlee, who believes in me and in the message God has sent.
Hi Mom!

Contents

Preface

The Game

Chapter 1
In the Shadow of Failure

Chapter 2
Starting Over

Chapter 3
Life by the Spirit

Chapter 4
Walking in Our Authority

Chapter 5
Subjection and Submission

Chapter 6
Being the Church

Chapter 7
The Religion of Me

Chapter 8
The Rest of God

Q&A

About the Author

Why a second edition?

There are a number of reasons that I thought about doing a second edition. As I matured in my faith and writing style it became clear to me that my earlier version contained too many bunny trails. The revelation of the Cross of Christ is still very much the central theme, but in this version I have been able to streamline subject matter and place focus on the most important points that a believer should come to know.

I hope you enjoy the new version.

Preface

Philippians 1:9-10 And this is my prayer: that your love may abound more and more in knowledge and depth of insight, so that you may be able to discern what is best and may be pure and blameless until the day of Christ...

I'm convinced that a new chapter in church history is about to unfold for those that have ears to hear. I'm also convinced that a wonderful journey is in store for the believer who can push past the "status quo" and any preconceived ideas about the Christian faith, in order to consider a way of life that more readily resembles our Savior.

If you are content with your faith, your church, and your Christian walk, then you don't need this book. However if you have ever found yourself taking a wrong turn in your pursuit of God, or you just lack assurances in your faith, then I invite you to participate in a refreshing and possibly life changing message.

I also want to encourage each believer to make this a personal journey. Be ready to speak to God with your own voice and in your own way about the concepts we are presenting. If you are unable to formulate your own words then you may find comfort in using the declarations or prayers that have been provided. The points listed in each came from my own personal journey into greater wholeness and fullness in Christ.

This book is not about doctrine as much as it is about growth, maturity, and transformation through a relationship with Jesus. In each chapter, you will be challenged and comforted while reevaluating what you believe about the Christian life.

*****

The Game

Eleven year old Nate had been fascinated with board games for more than half his life. He loved them because they provided him a sense of adventure and accomplishment. In addition they created a certain level of excitement when personal risk was involved. Yet for Nate there was also the sense he could control his mythological destiny.

Since all the games he owned had previously been conquered, he decided it was time to buy a new one. So as he made his way to the local toy store, he prayed under his breath for a chance to find a game so special that he could lose himself in its intrigue.

As he scanned the toy aisle, he spotted many of the familiar board games which he had stored underneath his bed, but then his gaze fell upon a game that he had never seen before. Picking up the box and tabling it against his stomach he snickered a little as if to mock the simplicity of its plain brown wrapper. "The Game" was written in bold letters with one additional line of print. It read, "The game that plays with you." In that a moment a subtle shock tantalized his senses, and Nate repositioned the box right along with his opinion. "I think this may be what I've been looking for."

As he approached the checkout counter he realized he had not given any thought as to the cost of the game. Flipping the box over many times he scrambled to find the price, but no price tag was in sight. It was then that the manager noticed Nate's frustration. To his amazement, the manager looked at him with a gleam in her eye and said, "The game is free."

Nate snapped to attention; "What---What did you say?"

"The game is free; please step to the right of the checkstand and have a great day!"

At first Nate didn't know how to respond. When he looked at the manager for some type of reassurance, she winked and told him to enjoy his gift. In that moment he began to glisten with excitement; it was as if he had just won the lottery!

With a proud grin on his face, Nate made his way through the exit door to the front sidewalk. As he basked in the summer sun and in the joy of his new treasure, an elderly man dressed in a clean but dated suit greeted Nate with a smile.

"That's a fine game you have there son," the man said softly. "I actually invented the rules for playing that game, and I just now purchased it with you in mind."

Nate looked back at the man and said, "There must be some mistake mister, I was given this game for free."

"No", the man said; "This is my store and I can make these types of decisions"

Nate turned to look back to the store manager for a confirming nod, but the manager's attention had already been given away to another customer. Within that very moment the elderly man fumbled his cane to the ground and implored Nate to fetch it for him all the while the man chatted away about the game, as if to confirm he really had invented it. As Nate stooped down to rescue the fallen cane, a puzzled look crossed his face. The joy of the moment faded a little as he sensed there might be a catch; somehow he felt that "free" might not be so free after all.

Once Nate had returned the cane, the old man explained that the game consisted of a board fashioned with one hundred squares in a grid pattern. Within each of the squares was a statement of truth that would lead players to realize a greater wisdom in their personal life.

"This is not just a board game son; it's a way to gain your richest rewards. Every great man on the earth has played my game. Even Jesus is well acquainted with my game and I can see that you too have the potential for greatness."

Nate studied the man's face and found no reason to doubt his sincerity. With a smile and a nod of agreement, he yielded to the old man's reason.

The pair walked the length of the store's front sidewalk and sauntered towards a wrought iron bench. Nate sat to the right of the friendly man and with eagerness readied himself for more instruction.

"I'd like to know more" he said.

The old man winked. "You came to the right place son"; and then began expounding on the rules of the game. He explained that within each square a player must sacrifice something of personal value in order to receive the fullest benefit from each statement of truth; the greater the sacrifice, the greater the return. A player's own dedication and sincerity would determine the cost, but the reward for commitment would be tangibly real. Advancement would bring honor and prestige for those willing to go the distance. Nate couldn't contain himself any longer; he was certainly primed to start playing.

"Is there anything else I need to know?"

The old man leaned toward Nate as if to inspire destiny.

"The only other thing you need to know son is this; the greatest achievement and the highest reward in this game will be to finally know who God is."

"Wow! I can't wait. Thanks, mister!"

Anxious feet now began to propel a body that hadn't even left the bench. When touch-down commenced, Nate ran with the gait of a stallion and the agility of a linebacker. The length of two city blocks seemed like a single leap for joy and a swirl of wind landed him at his front door. Bursting into the house he made his way up the stairs in only three hops. Dodging toys, balls and his baby brother, he bounded down the hall, exploding into his room and flopping onto his bed.

With his body now perched on the edge of his mattress, Nate tore into the box as if he were looking for his heart. The board flew one direction, game pieces in another, and the instructions sailed out of the reach of a mind preoccupied with destiny.

Nate scooped up the game and his eyes slowly scanned the etched parameters of the board. There where gold gothic swirls upon its border, all of which enhanced a meadow of forest green squares. Like plots of land seen from above, each square was outlined with a fence of woven gold twine. Adjoining squares were also made regal by a raised ruby thumbtack inserted at each point of intersection and there were also words etched deep within each square kingdom.

Nate noticed that there was something familiar about the etchings and began to touch the surface of the board for confirmation.

"It's a verse; in fact they're all verses from the Bible!" Nate exclaimed.

He knew these verses or at least he knew they were scripture." His hand continued to brush across the surface as if he were trying to feel truth for the very first time. Then he remembered, the old man had said that all the great men of the world had played this game and it would bring wisdom and honor to whoever played it.

Whispering to himself he asked, "What did the old man know that the scriptures didn't say?" "That's right; he also said that playing the game would bring me fame and most importantly I would then be able to know God. The old man must have been seeing something that only years of wisdom could reveal". In that moment Nate fully committed himself to the game.

He flattened the sheets of his unmade bed in an attempt to ready an acceptable game table. Positioning the board in the center of the bed, he then carefully selected a royal crown as a fitting game piece. As he placed his marker onto the first square, he sensed a unity with all who had gone before him. A rush of adrenaline left his hand shaking as he released himself into a journey of incomparable mystery. Commitment now was perfectly joined with destiny as he read the first verse with a slight quiver in his voice. The game had commenced.

"If any of you lacks wisdom, he should ask God, who gives generously to all without finding fault, and it will be given to him. James 1:5"

"I see the value in what the verse is saying. God probably thinks that wisdom is pretty important. I will look for a sacrifice, which is generous and worthy of wisdom."

Nate looked to the shelf above his desk that displayed his collection of car models. He'd spent many hours cutting, sanding, and painting. Great attention to detail had made his models the envy of his friends; they were trophies that certainly brought him joy. With a sense of exhilaration Nate proceeded to make his first personal sacrifice. Choosing his 57 Chevy, he carefully cradled the model in his hands and placed it in a shoe box for delivery to his best friend Frankie. Nate smiled with delight. The old man was right; there was a sense of honor and prestige in playing the game. How many other boys his age could say that they had made such a sacrifice for the privilege of pursuing God? Nate proceeded to advance to other levels with the same enthusiasm and each move seemed to provide him a greater sense of reward and accomplishment. He began to understand what the old man had talked about regarding the gratitude and admiration of friends.

With each sacrificial gift he thought back on the old man and wished he could share with him the joy of each victory.

As night fell, Nate had made considerable progress. Thirty squares had revealed thirty verses of unparalleled wisdom. The thirty verses were now accompanied by thirty sacrificial toys that stood as a testimony to his commitment and pursuit of God. He breathed a sigh of relief as he looked at the vacancies on the shelves of his bedroom walls. An overwhelming sense of fullness radiated from his heart as he pondered all that had happened. With thoughts of the next day's strategy, he fell into a deep sleep.

As a new day began so too was signaled a new zeal. It was obvious that he had already experienced the honor and prestige due a person committed to giving away his possessions. Nate's generous donations also captured the attention of his friends. They were impressed by his dedication to the game, and keenly interested in what else he would be willing to sacrifice.

As Nate continued to unload the things that were special to him, his best friend Frankie became curious about what had brought on this behavior and asked; "Why are you giving things away for the right to read bible verses?"

"You don't understand, Frankie, there is so much more to this game than reading verses. The game is about life. It allows me to gain things that you can't get by just reading the Bible. There is a thrill in risking everything, but the best part is I will also get to know God."

Frankie said, "Well, I know God and I don't have to give things away."

"Maybe you know God, but God is more real and powerful, and he likes you better when you sacrifice things. Besides, the man who created this game chose me to receive it absolutely free." Nate said proudly.

Frankie looked around the empty room with raised eyebrows and with a cautious tone he mumbled under his breath, "It sure doesn't look free to me."

Nate snapped to attention and then stared at Frankie trying to generate a verbal comeback. He stumbled with his thoughts and then finally said, "If you had sacrificed as much as I have for the Bible and the right to know God, we could be best friends!"

Frankie looked surprised. "How can you say that we would be better friends?"

An awkward moment of silence filled the air and then Nate pointedly exclaimed. "Just leave me alone if you aren't willing to commit to the game!"

Frankie turned and began to exit the bedroom door. With a quiver in his voice, he said, "We are already best friends, and Jesus has already saved you."

For a split second, Nate disengaged from the old man's instructions and remembered things that were supposed to last forever, like friendship. But he quickly realized that he couldn't return to the way things were; too much had been given away without a venerable pay-back. He thought to himself, "If I quit now I would be laughed at and have nothing to show for all my efforts. I would also lose the honor that comes by finishing the game. My only hope is to keep going on until I find out what the old man knew to be true. " In an attempt to encourage himself Nate then proclaimed;

"No one else has seen what I am about to see, because no one else is willing to do what needs to be done in order to win. Nate then prayed harder then he had ever prayed before. "God, I know you want to be found. I have many squares left before I reach my goal of knowing you. If you have shown this old man the truth about how to make that real, then I want it." It was at this point that Nate looked around the room and was astonished to realize he didn't have much more to give away. He then jumped up and ran to his closet and found it empty. He rummaged around his dresser drawers, trying to recall where his bug collection was; then he remembered that he had already given it to Peter. He foraged through the chest against the wall; still nothing of value. He lifted the blankets to look under his bed; yet all that was there was a bunch of old games.

With a sunken feeling Nate realized that these old games were all he had left. With dwindling hope he began to count them: One, two, three…ten…. fifteen… FIFTEEN! Anguish gnawed at Nate's heart and in panic he realized his dilemma.

"I don't have enough! I can't finish … I can't finish the game!"

Reflecting back Nate began to recollect all that it had cost him to play the old man's game. "God, I gave away seventy things of value in order to find you, and here are another fifteen. If I had watched my giving, maybe I could have finished the game. Please God, don't let this happen! Surely there must be a way that I can still find you? Could you at least share a part of yourself with me, maybe the part that is worth 85 gifts?"

With a sigh, Nate began to finish sacrificing his last fifteen possessions, hoping that God would some how respond to his incomplete, but sincere commitment. Looking for a miracle, Nate then cried out, "Please God, what must I do? Show me the way so I can finish the game and know you."

With no answer from heaven Nate braced himself for the inevitable conclusion. Down to his final five squares, he then read the next verse;

The Spirit of the Sovereign Lord is on me, because the Lord has anointed me to preach good news to the poor. Isaiah 61:1

Nate thought to himself about God's anointing on Jesus' life and then decided on his best choice for a sacrifice; "This will have to do as payment." Advancing in another move Nate reads:

Heal the sick, raise the dead, cleanse those who have leprosy, drive out demons. Freely ye have received freely give. Matthew 10:8

As he pondered the greatness of Jesus' ability to heal the sick and raise the dead, he wondered what leprosy was. "I'll pay for healing with this game over here." Still he read another.

There is no difference for all have sinned and fallen short of the glory of God, and are justified freely by his grace through the redemption that came by Christ Jesus. Romans 3:23&24

What should I then pay for justification and redemption? I'll give this game over here. Nate then read his fourth verse

We have not received the spirit of the world but the Spirit who is from God, that we may understand what God has freely given us. 1 Corinthians 2:12

The Spirit…what should I pay for that?

Nate now sat on the floor with two games in his hands. He began to ponder his dilemma and realized that his two worst games were all he had to give.

"God, what should I do?" What can I do to make you happy? How will I please you when I don't have anything left to give?"

Nate sat in a stupor for a moment and then it came to him; "The old man, he will know what to do!"

Bolting from the house, Nate made his way back to the store where he had met with the old man. A quick scan of the store and the grounds revealed no old man in sight. Nate exclaimed, "Just when I need answers the most, I can't find him; there must be a way to locate him." He then remembered that the old man had said that he owned the store, so Nate went to find the manager. "Please, lady, can you tell me where I can find the owner of the store? I was talking with him the other day and he bought me my game."

"I remember you," the manager said. "You were one of the prize winners in our Saturday promotion. How's the game?"

"The game was fine until I couldn't finish it. I was looking for the old man who owns the store. He was the one who told me all the rules and I thought maybe I'd misunderstood something he said."

"What old man? There's no old man here, and he certainly doesn't own the store; this store is owned by a big company."

Nate steadied himself against the checkout counter trying to catch his breath. After he regained his composure, he asked the manager, "You mean I did win the game after all, and it was free?"

"Yes, it was our anniversary sale and there were winners throughout the day; your game was free."

In a dazed state Nate staggered out of the store and stuttered, "What has happened to me, all I wanted was to know God?"

As he looked toward the parking lot, he spotted the old man. "It's him! I'm sure of it!" Nate's heart jumped and then compelled his feet to move. As he crossed the parking lot, he made eye contact with the old man and spouted, "You lied to me about the game old man! You promised me I would receive honor and prestige and wisdom if I gave all my stuff away. The old man looked at Nate and slowly he replied, "Why, son, that is not quite true."

"Yes it is true" Nate barked! "You promised me!"

The old man calmly sat himself on the base of a lamppost, his posture suggesting a conversation that he has had a million times before. "You say that I promised you honor and prestige and wisdom? Is it not true that your friends respected you when you handed them gifts? The greatest men on the earth desire such respect."

Nate's lip began to quiver and an astonished look came upon his face.

The old man continued. "Did you not learn the value of giving away all that you had, in order to decide that giving wasn't enough? Men have sacrificed more without a single return on wisdom. I told you the truth."

Nate's shoulders slumped and he looked to the ground in defeat. The old man's argument was too much to bear. With brokenness in his voice Nate responded in exhaustion, "All I wanted was a game that brought me a little more excitement, and you made me give all my things away; I even lost my best friend Frankie."

With a painful look on his face Nate exclaimed, "You not only stole my happiness, but I thought I was going to get to know God?"

"God!" "You are still wondering about god? Have I not proven to you that I am he? With everything that motivated you to play the game, have I not proven to you that I can deliver? Does that not make me god?"

Nate looked at the old man with astonishment, his eyebrows creased towards the center of his forehead and with a soft voice he said:

"No, --- I mean ------------ "God."

The old man's cane began to shake as he grasped tightly upon the handle. He stood, straightened his coat and proceeded to exit the conversation.

"I can promise you all the wealth of the world, I can position you for greatness in any land, and I can even guarantee you political or ecumenical achievement, but delivering you "GOD" is not my GAME!"

Determined to end all rebuttals, the old man turned and walked away. Nate's clueless expression proved that he had no idea what had just happened. With a scrunched up face he made his final assertion.

"Mister, you're WEIRD!"

As Nate made his way home, he felt a little better even though he knew he was going to have to face the inevitable reality of his decisions. Again, Nate called on God to help him deal with the burden. "Jesus, I'm still hurting, and I still need you to answer me. How can I know you when so many rules seem to stand in the way? If it isn't rules about a game then it's rules about life. Please help me."

Nate returned to his room and plopped down in the middle of the floor. Looking at the game that had cost him so dearly he tried to determine what had happened.

"How could I have paid so much to play a game?"

As he stared glassy eyed into oblivion, he noticed a white piece of paper tucked upright at the far end of the closet. Reaching for the paper, a thought captured Nate by his heart. It was the rules to the game! When he opened the folded paper, almost immediately that sunken feeling was gone. A single verse explained in a second what Nate had forgotten and what an old man didn't understand. It read;

It was for freedom that Christ set us free; therefore keep standing firm and do not be subject again to a yoke of slavery. Galatians 5:1

Instructions for playing "The Game"

Memorize as many verses as you can. With each verse memorized you get to move your marker forward. Play with all your friends or just play with God. God and His word will never leave you.

Game pieces:
1- Game board,
6- Markers
1-Holy Spirit included!

Introduction

After forty years of Christianity, I came to the conclusion that I had somehow missed the way. Recalling the spiritual journey that had summed up my life, I realized that there was very little fruit to prove that all my striving for God had paid off. My dilemma came from a sense that He wasn't available to me as I believed He could be. This nagging thought demanded answers; was He really there, or had I spent four decades believing in some ethereal image of a savior? Now, my heart knows Jesus exists and I've seen Him move in times of crises, but I really needed to know whether there was more. Was there any proof we actually had gained a relationship? I could sit in a church and be aware of the presence of God all around, however I was never sure if He was making Himself known because He loved me, loved the leader, the choir, or maybe it was the pew that I was sitting on. Without some greater assurance I felt like little more than a rescue mission.

About this time there seemed to be a breath of fresh air. I was introduced to a small group of believers and a very charismatic leader. They appeared to be dedicated Christians who really loved God and were committed to looking for what could be called "the deeper Christian walk." Our first prayer meetings on Wednesdays were so successful and encouraging that within a short time we were soon meeting together most every night. It was an expression of church life and fellowship I had never seen before.

These people were different because they were not content with the Sunday church mindset; instead they wanted to know what it meant to "be" God's church. In their motivation they were looking for ways to invite Jesus into their daily lives and gain a true understanding of both intimacy and maturity. At the time this appeared to be a healthy example of fellowship, unity, and spiritual practice all leading to that one goal. I was convinced that the greatest expression of godly relationship was seemingly staring me right in the face and I certainly didn't want to miss out on any of it. Under their direction I was ready to prove myself as available, capable, and reliable to the God that supported their faith.

Five years of commitment passed quickly and brought me to the place where the gentle voice of the Holy Spirit was calling me to move on. There was a sense that another aspect of His life was just on the horizon and that meant moving away from the security of this small group; however my choice was met with disapproval.

As I proceeded to make plans to leave, I was confronted by a feeling of alienation. Suddenly, the people who had been near and dear to me began to pull away. The word had gone out that I was now off limits to anyone who still desired a committed Christian walk. If that was not enough of a rude awakening, there was also a real and foreboding sense that God Himself had some how left me. It was as if someone had pulled the plug on a dynamic spiritual connection and I was now empty, confused, and very much alone.

How could this be? How could I know God in such a great and powerful way in one moment and then seemingly find such a cataclysmic lack of His potency in another?

After much thought I came to the conclusion that I had not actually invested in a true relationship with God after all, but had been overly dependent on others for my Christian walk. My error in judgment went back even farther than this last group of believers. I realized that throughout my entire Christian experience I had sought out qualified mentors and then mimicked their spiritual success as a sign of Christian devotion. However to depend on others for the answer when I had been granted my own access to the one true God was tantamount to spiritual suicide. Said in another way;

Because I didn't go to God first, confusion dominated much of my Christian walk.

Yes, Jesus had made Himself known to me in salvation, but like the eleven-year-old boy, I hadn't taken the time to read the instructions. The result was an improper trust in man to move me along in my faith rather than a healthy dependency and trust in what Jesus could deliver all by Himself.

This pattern of improper dependence on others is not mine alone and can be found in most every religion on earth. What is created are all sorts of disconnected religious agendas, each one proclaiming that they must be the one true way.

I then started to look more closely at the subject of Christianity. Was there a reason that the Church was also so divided? Shouldn't we be participating in a singular expression of Christ; so why all the factions? Then another question gripped my heart, "If the Church was so divided in their definition of true Christianity, could it be that I myself had missed a healthy foundation for knowing God?"

Is it possible that even in the Church I could have believed in another god?

This question was intriguing and at the same time scared me to death. To come to the conclusion that I may have not known a pure expression of Jesus was overwhelming. Based on that earth shaking inquiry I became motivated to find an answer, but where could I go for a clear perspective? That's when I came across something Paul the Apostle once wrote and it confirmed my suspicions.

2 Corinthians 11:3-4 But I am afraid that, as the serpent deceived Eve by his craftiness, your minds will be led astray from the simplicity and purity of devotion to Christ. For if one comes and preaches another Jesus, whom we have not preached, or you receive a different spirit which you have not received, or a different gospel which you have not accepted, you bear this beautifully.

Another jesus? A different spirit? A different gospel?

Paul was certainly speaking to me now.
This shook me to the very core of my being. Too many encounters with other men's gods had left me wounded, alone and falling headlong into religious delusions. In short order, I began to see how spiritually bankrupt I really was and I became frantic for answers. What I now needed more than anything was a way to make sure that the One True Savior was my only savior. For the first time in my life all I could do was cry out to Him for help.

"Jesus, I can't find you, would you come find me!"

What a powerful request that turned out to be. All my life I had been pursuing God, as if by my own strength and reason I could find Him. Yet He was able to make Himself known without my prompting. In this way, salvation and the continued unfolding of His plans could be His gift to me, rather than my religious obligation to Him. It would now be my highest call to wait upon Jesus and allow Him to be the one that adds true purpose, meaning and spiritual depth to my life.

Defining the Foundation

This transition was an important move for me. I was now determined to understand Christianity for myself. Christian ministry, practice, and doctrine where certainly a part of what needed to be looked at, but it really all hinged on whether I could first grasp the very basics of the Gospel.

Prior to this day I could have summed up the salvation message based on four spiritual laws.

- Jesus loves me.
- I'm sinful and separated from God.
- Jesus is the way for me to return to God.
- I must receive Jesus as Savior.

Yet this didn't answer the need within me for a continued move toward Christian maturity; a way to become more like Christ. To my amazement I was missing a significant piece of the puzzle. As it turns out a fifth spiritual law was necessary in order for me to put on the nature and character of Jesus. Galatians 2:20 brought this to light:" I have died with Christ."

Galatians 2:20 I have been crucified with Christ and I no longer live, but Christ lives in me. The life I now live in the body, I live by faith in the Son of God, who loved me and gave himself for me.

This scripture and many more just like it were stating that Jesus' death on the Cross was also the place of my death! No, I didn't die physically, but rather Jesus supernaturally took me into His own death so that I could also have access to His life.

Now hopefully you can see the benefit, but also the problem. Prior to this remarkable discovery I had spent too much time trying to make faith work; it had been my strength and discernment that was improperly calling the shots. I had inappropriately added rituals and concepts to my faith that eventually proved to be more destructive then good. These can best be described as agreements or contracts that had held me captive to a natural way of thinking rather than a trust in the mind and heart of Jesus. When this reality sunk in, I shook my head in disbelief because I knew I had given my authority away a hundred times over. Recognizing that all those choices were religious in nature and carried spiritual weight, I began to call upon the Holy Spirit to lead me out of the web of bad choices.

Talk About a Cure!
Romans 6:11(KJV) Likewise reckon ye also yourselves to be dead indeed unto sin, but alive unto God through Jesus Christ our Lord.
As a believer who had lost touch with Christian reality, I had many questions about how to get back to a simple faith. Those questions were soon resolved by the presence of a living and active Gospel. As the Holy Spirit prompted me to recognize my death with Christ I caught on to what He was saying: "Dead people are no longer owned by anything ---- especially bad contracts." If I have died with Christ then the strongholds that have once held me captive can fall away. All that was required of me was a willingness to let go of my past ideas about life, love and commitment and agree with His way of transformation. I promptly began to declare freedom from all sorts of issues that needed a redeeming breath from God.

"God, I recognize that I died with you to being improperly owned by this person, that contract (agreement) or that power.

Yet that is only half the benefit: once I let the Cross separate me from my former way of life, the resurrection power of God began to move in my heart, mind and actions. Jesus raised me up into a new and living way that was empowered by His Spirit.

God had just showed me the secret to the transformed life.

This one revelation became pivotal and changed everything I had previously known about the

Christian walk. It transformed a dead religion into a vibrant relationship with the Son of God and made me realize that only Jesus by His Spirit was able to bring this about.

Colossians 2:12b ... having been buried with him in baptism, in which you were also raised with him through your faith in the working of God, who raised him from the dead.

Romans 8:11 And if the Spirit of him who raised Jesus from the dead is living in you, he who raised Christ from the dead will also give life to your mortal bodies through his Spirit, who lives in you.

The delightful freedom I was now enjoying was the result of my death with Christ and His ability to make all things new.
In the pages ahead I want to tell you how I began to experience that freedom on a daily basis. It's a story that in part tells of my experiences with a small group of believers, but in reality it could just as easily be speaking of similar dynamics found in all of Christendom. A wonderful hope has been revealed in the Person of Jesus and there is not a day that goes by that I do not thank Him for leading me,

"Out from the Shadow of other Gods."

CHAPTER 1
In the Shadow of Failure

I lay on the empty floor of my apartment broken and confused. One hour had faded into three; three had turned into five, with no sign of an answer from God. I gasped for air, as if I could support my own ability to remain sane, but sanity had left me a long time ago; the choices I had made while in pursuit of God lacked any sound judgment.

What had gone wrong? How had I ended up so utterly destroyed when all I really wanted was more of Jesus? I wept as I reflected on the years that proceeded this moment.

The small group of believers had appeared so pure and zealous in their commitments. Having sought a deeper walk, their devotion and sacrifice rivaled that of most Christian's. Friendship and fellowship also appeared to run deep, but it all ended very abruptly.

Now I was convinced that my dedication to the cause should have proven to God and to men that I was the real thing. I sought for the Savior with abandonment and I let nothing interrupt my pursuit. But, in many ways there was nothing left to stand in the way. I had come out of an eleven-year marriage and had lost the family most dear to me. Within ten months I had also lost a promising career in retail. With nothing to pull me back into a structured lifestyle, I determined to commit myself to the goals of this radical group.

When I say, "radical" I'm not sure I can adequately describe the extremity of their commitment. They started off pretty normal, but over time it seemed as if greater degrees of devotion and sacrifice were required in order to satisfy their view of Christianity. If a person wanted to succeed it meant giving up most of the things that humanity had to offer. Under such a mindset, if you didn't give it away, you burned it or threw it against a cement wall. With every attempt at self-sacrifice came a belief that God would reward our dedication and commitment, but in reality we became very impressed with ourselves and our arrogance was appalling. The deeper Christian walk had taken a turn for the worse as the boundaries to healthy commitment and fellowship were lost.

Yet, when one is under such obligation, a question arises within the heart just like it did for the young boy in the story:

If knowing Christ is dependent on your giving, what happens, "Nate," when you run out of things to give?

I now know the answer; the free gift of God is "free"! But this does not solve the mystery nor unravel the dilemma I had put myself under. Yes, there had been some good times, but there was also a heavier burden than when I first arrived in the group.

In the last year of my association with this fellowship, God began to tell me that He would soon be moving me on. Conflict eventually surfaced when I brought up the subject of leaving and asked them if they had any insights. My request received mixed reviews. One associate spoke up and said, "Gee, we've never had anybody leave for good reasons before!" His statement was true, no one had ever left in the good graces of the group; it was always in the midst of disagreement. In the course of this conversation, the man who led this group finally made it clear he believed I was certainly deceived for even thinking of leaving.

Of course I was shocked! What was I to do? How could I honor my brothers and at the same time listen to the leading of the Holy Spirit? Who could possibly help me understand my dilemma and why was there a conflict in the first place?

After much prayer and personal soul searching, I finally determined that the Holy Spirit had truly asked me to leave. Yet, if I was deceived as the leader believed then at least I would be developing a trust in God alone. As much as I wanted to honor these friends I was convinced that Jesus had to remain my greatest counselor.

To my surprise I was now considered off limits to anyone who wanted to remain in the good graces of the fellowship. Friends and even roommates pulled away, driving home the point that I was no longer welcome.

This pronouncement stung with remarkable force. You see, I had made all sorts of commitments to these people and over the course of five years we bound ourselves to every type of religious agreement that we could think of. Though our vows, covenants and promises of loyalty and unity seemed right at the time, it was now clear that something was terribly wrong. And to confirm that there was a problem, I had now received the ultimate notice of failure. I had failed to remain within the confines of their vision and service to God. Was this truly Jesus at work in the hearts of believers? It was a question certainly worth exploring and as it turns out the answer has something to do with "free will"; or maybe we should say, "the misuse of it".

Free Will

The human heart seems to be geared toward conquering a natural world and that drive to succeed most likely began with Adam's early commission. When God created man He said to him: "Adam, you're in charge, so name the animals, be fruitful, and take dominion"; and Adam did just that. Then came a test of free will: "Adam, everything has been provided within this garden for you and your offspring. You have your physical needs met, you have a perfect wife and you can even walk and talk with me in the cool of the evening. However I have one request, stay away from THAT TREE!"

You know the rest of the story; a freewill choice to ignore the counsel of God got the first family kicked out of paradise. Once the fall took place they found themselves having to deal with:

- The loss of relationship with the Creator.
- The intrusion of the Serpent (the Devil) in their lives.
- Being subject to the Tree of the knowledge of good and evil.

The first represents the loss of a healthy friendship and resource of eternal counsel and security. The second introduced them to a foreign spiritual master. Yet probably the most life altering, day to day struggle for man would be in his bondage to the Tree of the knowledge of good and evil.

The Tree of the Knowledge of Good and Evil

Genesis 2:9 And the Lord God made all kinds of trees grow out of the ground, trees that were pleasing to the eye and good for food. In the middle of the garden were the tree of life and the tree of the knowledge of good and evil.

The Tree or Tree thinking is an important subject, due to its initial impact upon mankind's quality of life. Before the fall, man lived and moved and had his being within a physical domain, yet the glory of God was also present. That glory offered him a place to dwell in the righteousness and holiness of God. However when Adam and Eve partook of the Tree, they immediately began to trust "self" for all things (self-awareness). This poor choice obligated them to come up with their own brand of "right". In essence, if mankind's existence is not properly supported by the righteousness that comes from above, he will think and act upon his own perceptions of good and evil.

Actually a life built upon faulty good and evil standards is our problem. These two options for living have affected every generation since and have set improper boundaries for how we maneuver through life and faith. Sadly we are now obligated to continually juggle, balance and coexist with two conflicting streams of thought. Here are just a few good and evil concepts that we hold on to:

- Right and wrong
- Black and white
- Blessing and calamity
- Strength and weakness
- Success and failure
- Truth and lies
- Love and hate
- Mercy and judgment

Notice that whenever good is based on man's reasoning, he will by necessity make room for an equal and opposite response. Please don't misunderstand, certainly we should seek to support that which is good and shun what is evil. However when man is in charge of his own destiny he decides for himself the boundaries to what is good and what is evil and carries both in his heart. This good and evil practice creates a state of double mindedness. As the Apostle James points out: such a person is unstable in all their ways (James 1:8). Subsequently as they walk through life depending on their own dual conclusions they completely side step God's greatest provision.

You see, God isn't found in either of man's choices; He does not pattern success based on man's good and evil tree thinking. Instead He offers us a righteous standard that comes from above; one reflecting His own life, liberty and holiness. It is from this place of absolutes that God started to reveal His plans for the restoration of mankind.

The Faith of Abraham

First order of business was to show mankind abundant grace. So God approached a man named Abraham and offered him a remarkable eternal blessing.

Genesis 17:7 I will establish my covenant as an everlasting covenant between me and you and your descendants after you for the generations to come, to be your God and the God of your descendants after you.

The grace of God provided mankind an early access to a future Redeemer. What then followed was Abraham's trust that God could do, and would do as He said. God's character and preeminent nature revealed a promise that was supernatural and eternally life changing for Abraham and for all those who believe.

Romans 4:3 Abraham believed God, and it was credited to him as righteousness.
Gal. 3:9 So those who have faith are blessed along with Abraham, the man of faith.

In this way, faith in God became the key to mankind's restoration. However, there was still the need to deal with man's good and evil dance with the Tree.

The Old Covenant

430 years after Abraham, God established a covenant with the children of Israel which He delivered through Moses. The Law of Moses brought about a list of prerequisites which set mankind under certain obligations. In essence if man was going to define his way based on good and evil principles, then he would have to know that God had His own standard which needed to be upheld.

Deuteronomy 11:26-28 See, I am setting before you today a blessing and a curse— 27 the blessing if you obey the commands of the LORD your God that I am giving you today; 28 the curse if you disobey the commands of the LORD your God and turn from the way that I command you today by following other gods, which you have not known.

Not surprisingly, this redemption process became a heavier burden than the people could bear. The Covenant of Moses was a conditional agreement that could only remind the people that they fell short of God's perfection. Even today we see the significance of God's wisdom in this. The Law and its counsel prove that it is impossible for any of us to obtain favor by our own good behavior. The ultimate result for mankind is an awareness of sin and a large dose of failure.

The New Covenant

The Old Testament prophets spoke often of a future redeemer, one that would come and deliver them out of their fallen state. To make this happen, the Old Covenant had to be replaced with a new one. Following the law had revealed that we are a sinful people and if left to ourselves we will remain eternally separated from God. The only hope for mankind would be to find someone who could pay the price for our sin and represent us before the throne of heaven. It would have to be a man who had not given way to the same human examples of depravity, and one able to actually keep the requirements of the law. Yet because humanity had failed the test God had to provide His own redeemer.

The Father sent His only Son Jesus, made in the image of frail man, to take upon Himself the sin of the whole world. Where we were once held in contempt and eternally separated from a righteous Creator, God Himself provided us a way back into fellowship.

Hebrews 9:15 For this reason Christ is the mediator of a new covenant, that those who are called may receive the promised eternal inheritance—now that he has died as a ransom to set them free from the sins committed under the first covenant.

Jesus became man's source of righteousness, the heir of God's favor and the way in which we regain relationship with the Father. All that is required of us is a willingness to say "yes" to Him and embrace His offer of salvation.

2 Corinthians 1:20 For no matter how many promises God has made, they are "Yes" in Christ. And so through him the "Amen" is spoken by us to the glory of God.

Application
Jesus, I repent for my sin and accept you as the One who saves me and the One who restores me back into relationship with the Father. Yes God, I believe and therefore you credit to me your own righteousness.

The Law "In" Our Heart

For those now seeking to put on the life of Christ and bask in the grace of God we want to point out that the law didn't go away; God still believes in His standard of righteousness. However it is only by our intimate connection with Jesus that the law finds fulfillment in us.

Hebrews 8:10 This is the covenant I will establish with the people of Israel after that time, declares the Lord. I will put my laws in their minds and write them on their hearts. I will be their God, and they will be my people.

This affects us in three positive ways:
- God introduces us to His own righteousness. This is a gift obtained by the Blood of Jesus and allows us to approach the throne of grace without the threat of being condemned.
- The Holy and Righteous Spirit of God is set within us. This allows us to respond, not as one obligated to follow a rule book, but rather one being moved along by the nature and character of God.
- Thirdly the Holy Spirit becomes our ongoing counselor, leading us into all truth. When we remain pliable to the Holy Spirit's leading we gain insights as to what is good and pleasing to God.

These points provide a simple and effective means of interacting with God that create a holy and productive life; a life made in His image. However good and evil thinking can still interrupt our place of peace.

The Law of Our Heart

We know that the law was designed to show us a righteous heavenly standard and then bring us to a place of dependence on Jesus. As we finally realize that our abilities fall short of His ways our eyes get opened to just how desperate we are for Him to make all things right. Paul gives us a glimpse of this.

Romans 7:9-10 Once I was alive apart from the law; but when the commandment came, sin sprang to life and I died. 10 I found that the very commandment that was intended to bring life actually brought death.

The nature of the law brings death as well as assures us of eventual defeat. But Paul also saw how this law issue went far beyond the effects of even what Moses once preached. We have not only failed miserably in keeping God's law, but have also failed our own.

Romans 2:14-15 Indeed, when Gentiles, who do not have the law, do by nature things required by the law, they are a law for themselves, even though they do not have the law, since they show that the requirements of the law are written on their hearts, their consciences also bearing witness, and their thoughts now accusing, now even defending them.

This verse shows us that the law is more than just the written code. It can be any system of rules, regulations or principles which challenge us to seek after the Savior. Yet if the Savior doesn't remain the focus then we will tend to add more and more obligations to our lives in an attempt to bring balance. This unbridled effort to depend on ourselves and our own rules for success is called the "law of our hearts".

We understand from scripture that the law kills, but so too does the law of our hearts.

This issue is even more destructive than it first appears: if we leave the security of God's righteousness we will once again be obligated to measure success based on human principles. In Christ we have a perfect standard, yet apart from Him we each tend to live by the dictates of the Tree of the knowledge of good and evil. A question then arises;

Whose rules are we currently living by?*

If the law was so powerful that it brought death, then what can we expect from a myriad of improper good and evil human agendas? The bottom line is there are probably a thousand reasons why we end up failing the systems of men, but that failure has nothing to do with Jesus. However, coming to the end of any inappropriate good and evil game is a great place to be. It doesn't matter whether we have been assaulted by the Law of Moses or by some other form of obligation; in each case we finally get to put into perspective just how frail we are and how magnificent and gracious Jesus is.

Is it possible that God knew we were going to fail His standards?

Was He aware that the empty principles of this world would often condemn us? Did He know that we couldn't even keep our own rules? Sure He did, and in anticipation of our eventual defeat He provided us with a Savior and a way to gain a lifetime of second chances. Getting back to a place of peace and rest begins with a very simple confession.

God, I Was Wrong!

This is just a first step to something wonderful. As we confess our failure we are choosing to let go of any and all past ideas that may have improperly owned us. Take a minute or two and get alone with God. Tell him about the good and evil games you've been playing. In fact be ready to tell him how wrong you've been about being right! It doesn't take much to get God to show up when we are willing humble ourselves.

Please keep in mind we are not talking about the rules that govern society and keep us all from imploding. We are talking about unnecessary rules that are born out of man's fallen nature (His sinful, Adamic, old man, human nature) which deny us abundant life in Christ.

Application
Jesus, I was wrong to place so much faith in fallen good and evil principles, especially when your own standard of righteousness and relationship was made available to me right from the start.

Now if you are like me and failure has already marked many of your Christian endeavors, then maybe it is time to experience the joy of starting over.

Linda's Comments

As believers we have often formulated our own opinions about what is "right" and what is "good." We don't consider that compared to God's greatness we are woefully insufficient. Even when confronted by scripture proclaiming that our righteousness is like filthy rags, we have a hard time believing it.

"I was wrong" is one of the most profound statements of repentance. In those three words, we admit that even our best Christian effort and sacrifice does not measure up to the simplicity of God's goodness.

CHAPTER 2
Starting Over

As I became distanced from the small group of believers, the days passed by without any sense of real closure. I became increasingly aware that something was seriously wrong. Though I no longer interacted with them, I was definitely not free of their influence. I thought back on a bible verse which showed me the problem:

Colossians 2:8 See to it that no one takes you captive through hollow and deceptive philosophy, which depends on human tradition and the elemental spiritual forces of this world rather than on Christ.

About this time I was getting a glimpse of how flimsy my faith really was. Apart from initially accepting Christ I never actually continued to build upon His foundation. All too often I had blindly trusted men to lead me, thinking that they would provide for me a relationship and a spiritual place to dwell. Because of this improper level of dependence I sought to please men before recognizing my own place of acceptance in Jesus. I spent considerable time confessing and agreeing with their plans regarding the Christian life and quite often jumped into their "good" agendas in order to build the kingdom. Reality proved otherwise; if there had been any building going on then I had become the bricks and the mortar to another man's mansion.

This made me angry; I trusted these people to properly move me forward in faith. I thought," Look what you did! Look how you robbed me of all that I hoped for in Christ!" But about the time I got to the end of my inner rant, it was obvious who was at fault; the truth was I had no one to blame but myself. After all, I had known Christ personally; the Word was abundantly available to guide me and I possessed the Holy Spirit as my counselor. The truth sank in with finality: I was in this dilemma because I had wanted something of God, but I chose to go to men to get it.

Consider how subtle this effect can be on the Christian life. If I improperly depend on men to be my connection with God, then I will be tempted to live by their version of success and failure. Now that is not saying that they don't necessarily know the way or don't at times have great things to say; however I have been given a chance to discover my own place in the kingdom, simply by trusting in the indwelling Savior. I can learn about life and godliness from His perspective and He can then be the one that occupies my time and attention. Sure, I can still receive from others, yet by trusting Him first and foremost I am able to refrain from taking unnecessary religious detours that have the potential of shipwrecking my faith.

1 Timothy 2:5 For there is one God and one mediator between God and mankind, the man Christ Jesus,

Please keep in mind, each time you hear me speak of "religion" I am not talking about a participation in a healthy relationship with God. Instead I'm referring to every attempt by mankind to be right before Him and motivated by rules, regulations and rituals of their own making.

Religion can best be described as a search for God that is subject to man's own strength and definition of a savior.

As can be expected, if man seeks for salvation utilizing his own reason, he will often find a god and a religion made in his own image. It doesn't matter if he offers up a wonderful example of "thou shalt not and thou shalt do"; apart from Christ it will destroy any chance of gaining true success in the faith. This dysfunctional mindset stops seeking for relationship with God and starts looking for a hostage!

This was my dilemma: I had been spending my time jumping through the hoops of a faulty religion, and I needed to set at bay my previous obligations, commitments and expectations. About this time I started to question how I was going to get back to a sure foundation: how could I hope to unravel the intricate web of religious bonds that so thoroughly claimed ownership of me? How could I know what to keep and what to throw away? Where did truth begin and where did error take its place? The burden was overwhelming until I heard that gentle, eternal voice:

"Start over."

What; could I do that? How could I ... I mean, what would it look like if I did?

The more I thought about it, I realized that nothing prevented me from going back to the beginning. In fact, now that the option was presented, it made all the sense in the world to confirm what it was that I actually believed; sort of like going back to Jesus 101.

So, what did I believe?

By virtue of the fact that I was troubled in my faith it was obvious that I needed to find the truth regarding the Christian life. That required challenging my previous understanding as well as calling upon Jesus to redeem me from any error. It meant laying down a natural way of defining the Christian life and allowing the Spirit of God to finally lead me into all truth. I then prayed;

Jesus, I ask that you would test the quality of my Christian walk. I am tired of believing lies about who you are. I've tried so many times to make it work but I keep missing you!

As I prayed, I knew God was listening. From this simple place of beginnings, I started to believe that He could set within me a true standard; one not based on how men add meaning to my life but rather a trust that Jesus could now bring line upon line of truth to my walk without any distractions. This trust in "His ability" could then provide me a genuine place of rest and also define for me a true "relationship" with Him. This is where the God's Word became important to my quest.

I trust the Word of God even though I haven't always seen it in a true light. The Bible is a wonderful love letter for anyone that is seeking to draw near to the Savior. In its pages we find insights regarding His law, His kingdom and His love for His people; all of which resonate with His voice and character. When we open up the Word we are being offered answers about life and godliness from God's perspective. What the scripture reveals is in every sense of the word, His "contract" with mankind.

God's Contract

A "contract" is an agreement between two or more parties.
- It first describes one party's intention to offer service or possibly an example of performance.
- Secondly it describes another party's role within that same agreement.

God's contract with mankind can be interpreted in a very simple manner. In scripture we see that He wants to restore man back into fellowship, so He vows to offer up His own Son in order to seal the deal. Our part is then quite easy: by saying "yes" to Jesus a living and active relationship commences.

Now once this contract is received, we are then encouraged to go and read through the Bible's many finer points and provisions. In so doing we gain a greater understanding as to who Jesus is and who we are while in His care. For this reason I thought it best to anchor myself in what the Word had to say about Him.

My Renewed Interest in the Savior

The Gospel, (the good news) gives us a look into the life of Jesus and His Kingdom and offers us an opportunity to be a part of something that is eternal. His claims are not based on religious principles, good and evil formulas, nor are they based on man's definition of a savior. Instead they represent the nature of a Sovereign Lord; one that is accessible, available and compassionate. Here are some of His many attributes:

- Luke 8:26-39   He is our Deliverer
- John 1:1   He is the Word
- John 3:31-36   He is the Son of God
- John 14:6   He is the Way to the Father
- John 1:14   He is God
- John 1:29   He was a perfect sacrifice for sin
- John 3:16   He is our Savior
- John 4:49-54   He is our Healer
- John 6:5-13   He is our Provider
- John 10:1-18   He is our Shepherd
- John 20   He is Victor over death
- John 11:1-25   He is the Resurrection

When we say yes to relationship, this living, breathing eternal Person begins to affect our quality of life. This connection is unique and powerful because it touches us at the deepest level of our being, offering us a spiritual awakening.

Jesus is a Spiritual King, ruling over a spiritual kingdom and offering each believer a spiritual new life.

This amazing connection is the answer to having a productive walk with God. It's based on a trust that His spiritual and supernatural nature is able to reach out to us and make us complete. Even our commission as Christians finds its greatest purpose and meaning when we see ourselves as a spiritual "new creation" and not a part of the old man (the old nature). Yet this spiritual aspect of the believer and our eternal link with the counsel of God will forever remain a foreign concept to Adam.

Mankind was initially set within a natural world and called to prosper while using natural strength. Thus the human drive to take charge by natural means became the norm. Even today, due to our flesh and blood nature, we are prompted to live out much of our existence by the strength of our natural man. It is for this very reason that success is often perceived by how well we do in our flesh. Man uses his body, soul and spirit in order to create tangible results and receive tangible rewards. But this "self made man" attitude denies that there is someone greater who has a better plan for mankind's existence. What's lacking from Adam's view point is the ability to take his hands off of life and trust in an unseen God's intervention. If mankind ever intends to access eternity, and all that comes from above, he must access it by faith.

1 John 5:3-5 This is love for God: to obey his commands. And his commands are not burdensome, for everyone born of God overcomes the world. This is the victory that has overcome the world, even our faith. Who is it that overcomes the world? Only he who believes that Jesus is the Son of God.

From this place of trust (faith) we begin to discover a different way of defining success. All attempts at producing fruit for God must come by having a dependence on the Holy Spirit. It is only after we seek the Lord on His own terms that our humanity can effectively and productively respond. This should make us ponder the question:

"Has He really needed our help in order to make the kingdom work?"

And still a greater question worth asking is;

"Has He needed our help to make our Christianity work?"

If we are willing to challenge what we have previously accepted as the "Christian norm", we will discover that there has been a longstanding wrestling match taking place within the faith. An overzealous attempt to help God along has not produced a true reflection of Christ, but has added to the message and the work load. This isn't healthy, but rather it is a clear sign that we have usurped God's position as Savior. Thus, our inappropriate attempts to handle Christianity by natural means become a stronghold. This is where we are introduced to religion and relationship with God starts to fade.

By being natural in our expectations we strive to understand God from a human point of view. Answers that should have come by the guidance of God's Spirit get replaced with expectations that God is somehow going to cater to our fleshly assertiveness. This mindset reminds me of the religious zeal present in Paul the Apostle before his conversion.

Paul was a Pharisee of Pharisees: devout in his love for the law and the principles of the patriarchs. Due to his over zealous nature, he ended up persecuting the Church and missing out on the Messiah. It wasn't until God showed up and interrupted his plans on the road to Damascus that he began to see with eyes of full of faith. So if you can picture how driven Paul was in the defense of his religion, you might get a picture of how all mankind in general tends to promote and defend their beliefs. Yet Jesus still provides an easy yoke and a light burden if we want it.

Philippians 2:13 For it is God who works in you to will and to act in order to fulfill his good purpose.

Application
Jesus, I ask for a faith that originates with you, one that is as eternal as you are. I want a faith that trusts in your nature, character and Spirit.

Declaring our Faith

Understanding that Christianity comes from God's provision alone changes how we perceive the Christian life. If Jesus has His own ideas about life and godliness then we would do well to simply agree with His way in faith.

What we want to stress here is that everything related to the kingdom is complete and has already been given by the benevolent nature of a complete God. By holding onto Jesus, everything eternal becomes ours, and remains accessible as we trust in His balanced provision. This is also the place where our continued agreement with God is important to the growth and maturing of our faith. Paul reinforces this by saying:

Romans 10:9-10 That if you confess with your mouth, "Jesus is Lord," and believe in your heart that God raised him from the dead, you will be saved. For with the heart a person believes and so is justified, and with the mouth he confesses and confirms salvation.

The Greek word for "confess" in this passage is "homologeo" and is defined as: saying the same thing as another, i.e. agreeing with; conceding to confess, declaring; professing to declare openly, speaking out freely; praising and celebrating.* (Other scriptures that bring forth the same emphasis: Matthew 10:32, 1 Timothy 6:12, Hebrews 13:15)

This pattern of agreement should never leave us. Instead it should be a template for how we partake of every advantage known to the Christian life. To put it another way; our agreement becomes an effective prayer which gains God's immediate attention. When faith, truth and a right confession come together in Christ we will find a response from God every time.

*In the pages ahead look for confession, agreement and declaration to be used interchangeably to describe our agreement with God.

As we walk forward in faith we can also expect that the Spirit of God will be there to add the inspiration. In other words we need Him to be prompting us, if not challenging us, to respond to His leading. Without His unction we can quote scripture all day long, pray glorious prayers and even work our hands to the bone but for all the wrong reasons. Yet it is only after God opens our heart and our eyes to His ways that we become effective.

A great example of this change in perspective can be found in the following verse.

Matthew 16:15b-18 "Who do you say I am?" 16 Simon Peter answered, "You are the Messiah, the Son of the living God." 17 Jesus replied, "Blessed are you, Simon son of Jonah, for this was not revealed to you by flesh and blood, but by my Father in heaven.

A clear distinction between our works and His is what divides the Church in so many ways. In my own case, my clouded judgment required that I set aside doing and thinking "for God" long enough to gain a right perspective on all that He has done for me. Yet since many of my previous choices were obviously religious in nature, I also needed Jesus to teach me the way back to a true foundation. This is how I learned to walk by the Spirit.

Linda's Comments

We came from different places. Gordon began his journey from a position of desperation and I began mine from a decision to challenge what I had accepted as "normal" Christian practice. Overall I felt content and fruitful, but deep down I had an unsettling suspicion that I may have been adding an odd assortment of religious things to my faith that were not a true reflection of Christ.

At the time I had been a Christian for 38 years, in ministry as a counselor for 17, and a pastor for 5. Though all seemed well on the surface, I still couldn't say that my life and experience reflected the freedom and rest revealed in the Word of God. Standing at a safe distance, I watched my friend Gordon start over and the changes in his life encouraged me to take the risk.

"I started over". I asked God to take me back to the true foundation of salvation and relationship with Him, and He did! Since then I have found an even greater treasure in Christ without all the religious distractions.

Most people wait until they are desperate before challenging what is familiar and comfortable about their faith, but it is not necessary to burn out or break down to find the fullness of Christ; we can simply choose.

CHAPTER 3
Life by the Spirit

The New Day

What has happened to me? Where am I? It's so dark. Wait, I remember. I was crossing the street and that truck was just about to crash into me, but that's all I recall. Everything after that is a blank, and now I'm here, but I don't know where here is!

Lord, are you there?

Lord, I'm scared. Please, are you there?

Lord, please save me. SAVE ME LORD, SAVE ME!

I'm here, my child. I am with you always.

Lord, I was so scared! I thought I was all alone in this blackness. Where are we and what has happened?

I saved you from a terrible accident my child.

But why is it so dark in this place? Where are we?

Be at peace, my daughter. We are at rest. You have entered my perfect place of rest, so close your eyes and sleep. I have something to share with you when you awake.

The Lord's soft voice caressed the ears of the young girl and spoke to the deep recesses of her being. A dream began to materialize, and the daughter of God found herself surrounded by visions that brought forth a disturbing paradox. It was then that she was roused from her sleep.

What is that sound, Lord? It woke me from my sleep. I was dreaming so many memories of my life; a mesh of all that I have done. Now I do recall some of it; I was busy removing things from my life that displeased you. The burden of life was so very great, and I couldn't remember all that I had once yielded to and I felt weighted down. I'm worried, Lord, because it seemed so real. In the dream I exhausted myself under the weight of so much effort and the heaviness still seems to loom.

Lord, that sound is getting louder. Those visions were real, weren't they? Those events actually happened, and this wasn't a dream, was it?

No, child, it wasn't a dream.

Lord, I feel the darkness of those moments all around me now. It's as if there is no separation between me and the blackness. How can I get free of this and where does it end? It's as if every fiber of my being is one with this night. I have fought against this before; I have tried to escape it and it exhausted me and I now know there is no way I can ever leave its hold. I might as well be buried alive.

Buried? Buried alive!

Lord where are we and what is that sound? Please tell me!

The Father is approaching and is speaking my Name.

Oh no! He can't see me like this; He can't know that I am here! After all that I have done; after being joined to so much evil, He will surely judge me without mercy. His breath will consume me like straw, and the heat of His Holiness will obliterate me.

Lord, you have to help me. Hide me where black doesn't matter. Hide me where righteousness doesn't judge me with such finality!

Yes, my child, I have the perfect hiding place for you. But you must do as I say.

Please Lord, what must I do to be saved?

Feel for the wound in my side. Do not hesitate. Climb into my side and I will hide you there.

But Lord, how can I possibly enter so small a wound?

Quickly, tell me what it is you hold in your hands?

It feels like my life! How is that possible?

You have held it in your hands longer than you know. Begin to save yourself by throwing off all the burdens that you have become accustomed too. Do not hesitate, for the Father will soon be upon us.

I just threw down lust, pride and greed. I feel as if I'm getting smaller. There goes shame, and guilt.

Time is short; relinquish the rest of your load.

Lord, I think the load is gone, but I still can't seem to fit into your side.

Child, as you laid the burdens down, you believed you would enter the narrow way that was prepared for you. But there is more.

Yes Lord, but what is left of my life that could possibly be so black? I have removed all my sins and have become smaller in your sight, but I still don't fit.

What is still in your hand child?

My…my goodness; you want me to throw down my goodness? But, Lord, these deeds are the only things that prove I'm worthy of you. If I drop these things now, there is no gift for me to give to you, and there will certainly be no reward for my effort. If I throw these things down, I will surely die, for I have no other reason to exist! There must be another way?

At that moment the Lord increased the young saints understanding. Wait; Lord I see now; all this time I thought you were pleased with all the good works that I had accomplished. How could I have been so misguided as to think you would accept me based on my works rather than on your own? Oh, I was wrong Lord, I was so very wrong!

Child, what greater gift could you give than to simply be with me where I am? If your good works could satisfy the Father, they would have been accepted long ago. But all mankind has fallen short of My glory.

Lord, I'm ready now---------- I'm ready to give up and trust you, so that I can be with you; but I have a problem. There is a piece of my heart that would still try to prove to you and to the Father that I am capable. I can't lay down all my badness and I certainly can't lay down all my goodness. I need you to be my Savior, because I'm too strong in living, and too afraid in dying. Please, show me your way?

Child, what do you now know to be true?

I sense that this darkness is not all mine. I have entered into a place that contains all the good and evil that has ever come from mankind. And despite this awful darkness, somehow, I now know that I have already entered into your wounded side. I didn't have to make it happen. Now I am beginning to understand: it was the Cross! You took me into your death when you hung on the Cross!

Yes, child.

If you had not provided me a way in, I could never recover from God's judgment; but I'm at peace now. I am in perfect peace! Even though the blackest black is all around, I am no longer afraid because I am held within your love. And if night never ends then I am still safe in your embrace. If I had only known this while I was living.

You are about to be more alive than you ever thought possible.

Listen child…Listen.

Oh, Lord that's the sound of the Father.

He is coming to welcome us back from the grave.

With a cry from heaven, the Father cracked the tomb open to reveal the body of His only Son. All creation was now silenced by the matchless greatness of God's imminent presence. A thunderous voice beckoned the crucified lamb to respond. Four commanding words rolled across heaven and earth to awaken a lump of lifeless tissue.

Arise my Son! Arise!

In a moment, the power of God entered the tomb and breathed into the Son an eternal flame. Resplendent light, concealed before the foundations of the earth, passed between life and death to reveal a New Creation. A flash of love burst forth from the core of the Son of God, transforming all that was held within. For an instant a room of incomparable size was revealed where a multitude of joyous children began to glow with eternal light. Every molecule of lifeless tissue had just been made indestructible by the Fathers good pleasure.

Lord, I can see that it is now day.

Yes my Child,
> it will be Day
>> for a very long time.

The New Way
Romans 7:5 For when we were controlled by the sinful nature, the sinful passions aroused by the law were at work in our bodies, so that we bore fruit for death. 6 But now, by dying to what once bound us, we have been released from the law so that we serve in the new way of the Spirit, and not in the old way of the written code.

Unless we are brought up into God's ideas about life and faith we settle for a second best religion. That religion may look "good" on the surface, but it eventually fails to produce the life of Christ. Consequently we may need to separate from our good and evil choices.

But how does one stop being religious?

The naturally minded man would say; the way to freedom is to simply walk away from your troubles and don't look back. Yet our participation in religion is like a marriage: we have cultivated physical, emotional, intellectual and spiritual ties that continue and hang on until "death do us part".

Wait a minute; Paul used this same example when he described how we are freed from the Law.

Romans 7:1-2 Do you not know, brothers for I am speaking to men who know the law that the law has authority over a man only as long as he lives? For example, by law, a married woman is bound to her husband as long as he is alive, but if her husband dies, she is released from the law of marriage.

Our best efforts can't separate us from the trouble we have gotten ourselves into. Having been religious in our perspective means we have drawn to ourselves all sorts of natural and spiritual commitments that are contrary to the life of Christ. This is where our death "with" Jesus becomes so important to regaining freedom. It is also valuable for the ongoing care and feeding of the Christian life. The Word has quite a lot to say on this subject:

Romans 6:2	We died to sin.
Romans 6:3	We were baptized into His death?
Romans 6:6	Our old self was crucified with Jesus
Romans 6:7	We died and were freed from sin.
Romans 6:8	We died and are alive with Christ.
Romans 6:11	We are dead to sin but alive to God.

Romans 7:4	We died to the law through Christ.
2 Corinth 5:14	Christ died for all; therefore, all died.
Galatians 2:19	We died to the law to live for God.
Colossians 2:20	We died to principles of this world.
Colossians 3:3	We died, our life is now hidden in God.
2 Timothy 2:11	We died with him, we live with him.
Colossians 1:22	Reconciled by Christ's body through death.
Colossians 2:12	We were buried and raised with him

Notice that these verses are leading us back to Jesus on the Cross; they are also clearly written in past tense. This is because God offers us a complete redemption process and renewal based on what He did two thousand years ago. In fact all the promises of God, beginning with salvation, come from this one moment in time. Embracing this one truth becomes essential to gaining and maintaining victory in Christ: our identification with His death lets us leave behind our old man's ways in order to take up the free gift of God.

Understanding my death with Jesus became a life altering "eureka" moment. I knew in that moment that I was headed towards a remarkable season of transformation.

1 Corinthians 1:18 For the message of the cross is foolishness to those who are perishing, but to us who are being saved it is the power of God.

Let's look more closely at how this revelation can change our every circumstance.

- First, our death with Christ freed us from living under slavery to our natural man. The "old man" is a bigger influence than we care to admit. It is the power of man's soul attempting to define life and godliness on his own terms. Basically our "old man" is doing what comes naturally: he is lustful, he is full of pride, and he remains quite greedy. Natural man also believes that he knows the way to God; all the while still trusting in good and evil principles.

    Romans 6:1-3 What shall we say, then? Shall we go on sinning so that grace may increase? 2By no means! We died to sin; how can we live in it any longer? 3Or don't you know that all of us who were baptized into Christ Jesus were baptized into his death?

- Secondly, our death in Christ provided freedom from agreements that we made while subject to the old man's reign. These agreements were contracts that set the course of our lives and bound us up in physical, intellectual, emotional and spiritual ways.

Romans 7:5-6 For when we were controlled by the sinful nature, the sinful passions aroused by the law were at work in our bodies, so that we bore fruit for death. 6 But now, by dying to what once bound us, we have been released from the law so that we serve in the new way of the Spirit, and not in the old way of the written code.

- Thirdly, our death with Christ moved us outside of the limitations of the natural family and offered us a new heritage. You see the family we were born into was a by-product of our ancestor's good and bad choices. Family dysfunction, social disgrace, cultural repression, and issues of prejudice can leave lasting scars. Yet no past family curse or bondage still applies to us simply because we are now a new creation. We have been transformed by the power of God and we have been invited into a new family.

Ephesians 2:15-16, 19 by setting aside in his flesh the law with its commands and regulations. His purpose was to create in himself one new humanity out of the two, thus making peace, 16 and in one body to reconcile both of them to God through the cross, by which he put to death their hostility.
19 Consequently, you are no longer foreigners and strangers, but fellow citizens with God's people and also members of his household.

- Fourthly, our death with Christ allowed us to separate from the improper control of others. Not all faiths, beliefs or traditions lead to Jesus. However when we are subject to a religious box, other men's ideas, rules, regulations and obligations become a burden and a form of control. This is a place of "improper ownership" and alters how we respond in life and in faith. We can now challenge and find immediate freedom from these beliefs, traditions and bad contracts.

Colossians 2:20-21 Since you died with Christ to the basic principles of this world, why, as though you still belonged to it, do you submit to its rules: 21"Do not handle! Do not taste! Do not touch!"?

- Finally, man is a spiritual creature whether he serves God or not and that spiritual side of man is always looking for a connection. Yet a fallen world can only offer us imperfect spiritual resources. When we live like the world or remain naturally minded in our pursuits, unhealthy spiritual forces will influence and dominate us. Said in another way; if we are misguided in our ideas about God, a counterfeit spiritual realm is more than willing to jump into that role. But Jesus has already dealt with this matter at the Cross.

Colossians 2:15 And having disarmed the powers and authorities, he made a public spectacle of them, triumphing over them by the cross.

(Addressing this spiritual point of victory is something we will consistently bring before God since most of our choices include a spiritual element.)

When we died with Jesus, the covenants (contracts) that held us captive to all these issues were made void; they no longer have jurisdiction over a dead person.

<u>Application</u>
Jesus, I recognize that I died with you:
- **To living under slavery to my natural man.**
- **To agreements or contracts made while subject to my old man's control.**
- **To giving people improper control or ownership over my body, soul and spirit.**
- **To family dysfunction.**
- **To being subject to the devil and a fallen spiritual realm.**
- **To being the property of faulty religion.**
- **To being subject to any spiritual realm that supports these improper religious obligations.**

I know You are the Resurrection power that now saves me.

Raised With Him

Dead people also get to share in something marvelous;

Romans 6:4 We were therefore buried with him through baptism into death in order that, just as Christ was raised from the dead through the glory of the Father, we too may live a new life.

1 Peter 1:3 Praise be to the God and Father of our Lord Jesus Christ! In his great mercy he has given us new birth into a living hope through the resurrection of Jesus Christ from the dead,

These verses reveal how the Christian faith is unique and set apart from all other religions, it is the only one backed by "resurrection power". The Cross severs our bad contracts and the resurrection power of God then carries us on to completion. This is how we learn to walk by the Spirit. We don't have to live in the limitations of man's "good and evil" agendas; there is now a third option for living which is found in Christ.

Romans 8:11 And if the Spirit of him who raised Jesus from the dead is living in you, he who raised Christ from the dead will also give life to your mortal bodies because of his Spirit who lives in you.

This distinction between a life guided by natural rationale (man's sinful, Adamic, old man, and fallen human nature) and one guided by the Spirit can be seen in one of Paul's statements.

Romans 8:12-14 Therefore, brothers and sisters, we have an obligation—but it is not to the flesh, to live according to it. 13 For if you live according to the flesh, you will die; but if by the Spirit you put to death the misdeeds of the body, you will live. For those who are led by the Spirit of God are the children of God.

Please notice that Paul is confirming that there is a reason we include the Cross in our walk with God. Though it is often over looked Paul's message, testimony and ministry were saturated with a foundational understanding of death, burial and resurrection.

So how do we put things to death by the Spirit?

We simply come to the conclusion that Jesus has taken the misdeeds of our flesh into death with Him. The "misdeeds" we are referring to are any actions that still remain a part of our old man's ways. This can include any function in life or in faith that reflects the fallen nature; whether we do those things for bad reasons or for good. Once we have agreed with God it is then the Holy Spirit's job to bring about the necessary transformation for how we respond, in body, soul and spirit. The work of the Cross has already been accomplished but God has been waiting for two thousand years for us to agree with Him and His power to save.

Oh no! When this death, burial and resurrection Gospel finally sank in it wrecked everything I had previously known about my Christian walk. If my death with Jesus was so necessary in explaining the Christian life, then most every step I had ever taken within the veil of worship, service, ministry, devotion and comprehension may have lacked a proper trust in God.

What! You mean that there is a possibility that all my years of serving God were in vain because I thought I could make it work by my own strength?
Yep!
You mean that God didn't value my good and evil doctrines and theology because they were based on natural wisdom?
Yep!
You mean salvation hasn't been working because I thought it was all about me?
Yep!
The first option was to ignore the importance of this message and go on as if nothing had happened. I could return to my previous religious ways, and no one would be the wiser. The second choice was to admit that I had been religiously serving myself and others all these years and to cut my spiritual losses. Oh I was still saved, but I had become steeped in ideals that held me captive to a lesser quality of life and faith. I winced at the thought of relinquishing all my good works, but luckily Paul was able to confirm that I was on the right track.

Philippians 3:8 What is more, I consider everything a loss compared to the surpassing greatness of knowing Christ Jesus my Lord, for whose sake I have lost all things. I consider them rubbish, that I may gain Christ.
My desire for Jesus had yet to carry me into a sincere faith and my actions had created a back log of unnecessary religious obligations

and expectations. I had actually become a slave to them and as a result I was being pulled in a direction that was contrary to the will of God. This could have been terribly defeating, because I was already physically, emotionally and spiritually exhausted. Yet now I had at my disposal God's remarkable way of escape and I didn't need to remain bound and under any inappropriate load. By challenging the validity of every previous good or bad religious choice, I was inviting the Holy Spirit to support a new work in me.

Application
Jesus, I recognize that I too have been crucified with you. I no longer live, but you live in me. The life I now live in the body, I live by faith in you as the Son of God, because you loved me and gave yourself up for me.
Jesus, show me the benefits of my death with you, so that I can come to know your resurrection life.

I can only describe this process as incredibly freeing. Although this was just a "generic" declaration, I already understood its value! I also understood that there would be more to follow as I applied this understanding to other aspects of my life. In a nutshell, I had learned that forty years of Christianity was about to be renovated by a new landlord, and He was making it very clear that the best course of action was to get my natural man out of His way.

Linda's Comments
As a pastor, I tried diligently to simplify what I taught by going back to the basics. I wanted to present a Gospel that was all about Jesus; one that encouraged people to have an intimate relationship with Him. My desire was for people to focus on Him but it seemed to always end up being about us; our passion, our complacency, our pursuits, our interests or our indifferences. I didn't realize that one of the most essential basics was missing from all the teaching that I had received and delivered; it was our death with Christ. I had never known how to consistently walk in the Spirit because I had never understood that to know resurrection life required that I first be dead. This one truth was the key to finally letting it be all about Him and it has changed my focus as a pastor and as an individual. I now have true life to share with others and a Gospel that has become so clear that it burns in my heart and I can't help but share the good news.

How to Teach a Dead Dog New Tricks

I have absolutely no doubt that every part of our being can benefit from this way of transformation. So how do we begin to bring issues to Jesus? We can start with a generalized declaration or prayer.

When the disciples asked to be taught to pray, Jesus prayed a very general prayer. He said: "Father, thy kingdom come, thy will be done on earth as it is in Heaven". This generalized request gave the Father freedom to influence life and faith in the broadest sense of the word. It might be good to start with a similar prayer.

Father, thy kingdom come, thy will be done in my life and in my faith.

We can also start requesting that God look deeper into the issues.

For example, at the time I was struggling to see consistent godliness in my Christian walk. So I thought it best to start asking Him to decide for me what was "proper and improper" about my faith. If my improper choices had caused me to fall into disorder I needed Him to uproot every lie, but also preserve what was precious and true about my faith. As it happens only He knows how to separate the genuine from the counterfeit. By letting Him decide what was proper or improper regarding my worship, service, doctrine, relationships and ministry I saw significant change take place in how I responded to Him and to life in general.

<u>**Application**</u>

Jesus, I recognize I died with you to being able to know what is proper or improper;
- **About my faith.**
- **About my relationships.**
- **About my spiritual connections.**

Name some specifics regarding each as God brings them to mind)

I declare that You are the Resurrection power that now saves me.

This also prompted me to think about how I had been placing too much emphasis on my own ability to discern. Because I had been stuck in my own search for answers I was inappropriately deciding what I should bring near to my faith and what I should reject. This was Tree thinking in action, but specifically it was my drive to push forward to obtain things and then pull away when my initial choices failed me. This game never let me rest from all my striving and it also never lets me see Jesus as the Answer. The brunt of it was, I had been trying to be my own savior and that hadn't turned out so well.

Application
Jesus, I recognize I died with you to my ability or inability to manage life and faith and to accurately decide what I should draw near and what I should push away from;
- **In my faith.**
- **In my relationships.**
- **In my spiritual connections.**

(Name specifics regarding each as God brings them to mind)

There was also the opportunity to challenge how I viewed God's ability to function in my life. Was I holding onto a wrong perception of Him due to my previous religious beliefs? I then asked God to challenge my ideas about what is "possible" or "impossible" in Him.

Application
Jesus, I recognize I died with you to my religious ideas, and that of others, regarding what is possible or impossible in you.

This was just the beginning of a wonderful unraveling process where various limitations in my thinking and actions were removed. Once God began to release me from some of these generalized matters, He was then able to show me finer points that needed to be looked at. This progression, first dealing with general matters and then with specifics, has allowed me to find freedom from all sorts of improper contracts.

God's contract of salvation breaks all the bad contracts we have made; even the ones we thought were "good" for us

Now a question is set before each of us: if our death with Christ is powerful enough to break bad contracts and bring about greater freedom, then how much of our lives will we allow the Spirit of God to renew? Whenever the opportunity presents itself, I am now delighted to lose my dependence on the religion I once owned. (Actually there have been many opportunities to be religious). It may sound funny, but I always longed for Christ to be free in me, yet I kept allowing more and more barriers to be raised. When I finally did surrender I gained friendship, restoration, relationship and a place to dwell in Christ.

Unless we are willing to let go of our improper control of Christianity we will continue to spin our religious wheels.

Application

Jesus, I recognize I died with you;
- **To my dependence on my old man's choices regarding life and faith.**
- **To being subject to bad agreements or contracts which bind me physically, intellectually, emotionally and spiritually.**
- **To having my own religion that has added improper obligations and limitations to my walk.**
- **To having a religion made in the image of men, organizations, and a fallen spiritual realm.**
- **To being subject to any spiritual realm that supports these improper religious obligations.**

I declare that You are the Resurrection power that now saves me.

You actually have at your disposal the simplicity of the Gospel, which declares that you died and Jesus now lives. If you never read another page, but trusted the message, God is able to renew you from the inside out. All that is required is a willingness to let God bring exposure to bad contracts in your life; admit when you are in error and agree with His way of escape. The rest is then up to Him. By trusting Him first and foremost there are unlimited opportunities to grow and mature in the knowledge and counsel of God. It also establishes in us a true standard of authority.

CHAPTER 4
Walking in Our Authority

The title "Walking in Our Authority" may be misleading in part; the true question that needs to be answered is; "whose authority are we walking in?" As New Covenant believers we should be looking for a foundation that is commissioned and sustained by God. There are actually two types of authority that are spoken of in scripture. Let's describe both, beginning with Adam.

Adam's Authority

God initially offered Adam dominion on the earth. His intention was for man to rule and reign as master of his own domain. This commission began with man having authority over his person in body, soul, and spirit.

The Body... is Adam's physical structure. Made by God's design, the body possesses traits and characteristics that demand the respect of creation. The body exerts physical strength and ability which allows man to reproduce after his own kind. He also defends and maneuvers with physical prowess, achieving success by the work of his hands.

The Soul... is the essence of man's character and personality; this includes his thoughts, reason, and communication; it is comprised of the mind, will, and emotions:
- **The Mind** is the center of all voluntary and involuntary thought. It is the central processor for all bodily activity and is designed to process, compute, dialogue, and communicate on behalf of the whole person.
- **The Will** represents man's determination to choose his way and then bring that choice to completion; this describes "freewill". Once man deduces a plan of action his "will" is what maintains a commitment to that endeavor.
- **Emotions** express an immediate response to life and they provide us awareness regarding whatever touches our person. Emotions often let us know where our heart and our head are at. They often impact decisions in advance of a choice and can also keep supporting a decision long afterward.

These three aspects of the soul describe what is often referred to as "the heart of man" or the center of his being, yet this reference should also include a connection with man's spirit.
- **The Spirit...** is the essence of life. When God made Adam, He breathed into his body a living spirit, which made him a living creature. Man's spirit allowed him to communicate with God as well as have a general sense of spiritual awareness.

The body, soul and spirit represent the seat of man's authority, but that sovereign position also gives mankind an opportunity to influence the world around him. Authority then extends its reach relationally.
- As he embraces family life we see the emergence of "domestic" authority.
- As families are gathered together in community we see the formation of "social" authority.
- As these communities prosper into nations we see governmental authority established.

In a once perfect environment these various commissions would no doubt have shined bright with the glory of God and allowed mankind to succeed at whatever he did. They also would have taken advantage of the safety that existed while under the umbrella of God's own rule (Theocracy). However the fall of mankind, brought about the loss of personal authority and it polluted his true commission and calling.

Authority Lost

When Adam and Eve sinned, their actions created a separation from God. As the glory of God left them, so too did the godly compass that once inspired them to make right choices. The absence of God's goodness and holy character brought about self-awareness and as a result, self centered motives began to dominate their life style. Selfish reasoning and a distorted perspective became the barometer for what they would deem as good and evil. This caused them to lose touch with reality and their pursuits, both natural and spiritual, suffered for it.

It was the spiritual side of man that caused the most concern. Man's natural spirit lost a godly link. Without a proper connection with the Spirit of God, he looked for another spiritual resource. In the interim the Serpent or the Devil became a substitute savior.

1 John 5:19 We know that we are children of God, and that the whole world is under the control of the evil one.

Much more will be said on this subject in the next book, yet for now we will benefit in understanding that a different spiritual master is ordering mankind's steps and is often influencing how he functions in physical, intellectual, emotional and spiritual ways.

How does this apply to us as believers?

We still have our original commission from God and its O.K. to be human, but a trust in fallen principles will distort a person's search for Christian success. The good news is we've been given a second chance and what Jesus did on the Cross brought about a new standard of personal authority for all believers.

Authority Won

When Christ became our Savior, we gained an advantage not available to the natural man. We became part of a spiritual new creation, one with rights and privileges that are ordered by God. The new creation came about as Jesus passed our previously dysfunctional lives through the work of the Cross; His death, burial and resurrection became the place of our death, burial and resurrection. This one event is what separated us from the god of this world and brought us into the life of the Savior; we literally found a new place to dwell and an eternal intimate connection with God was formed. Here's an example of how close and intimate we now are to God.

John 17:22-26 I have given them the glory that you gave me, that they may be one as we are one: I in them and you in me. May they be brought to complete unity to let the world know that you sent me and have loved them even as you have loved me. "Father, I want those you have given me to be with me where I am, and to see my glory, the glory you have given me because you loved me before the creation of the world. "Righteous Father, though the world does not know you, I know you, and they know that you have sent me. I have made you known to them, and will continue to make you known in order that the love you have for me may be in them and that I myself may be in them."

These verses give us a glimpse of God's intended bond between Himself and the believer. Two remarkable positional truths are at work here when we come into union with Him.

First, the New Covenant provided the Spirit of God a place to dwell within a temple not made by the hands of men. What have we gained by such a design? It is nothing less than the power, presence, and purpose of God residing within pots of clay.

2 Corinthians 4:6-7 For God, who said, "Let light shine out of darkness," made his light shine in our hearts to give us the light of the knowledge of the glory of God in the face of Christ. But we have this treasure in jars of clay to show that this all surpassing power is from God and not from us.

For the record the New Covenant doesn't reveal a super human as some have anticipated. Instead, it reveals God's ability to do the miraculous with dirt. What God has done is set His Spirit within us as a guarantee that we should now belong to Him. The Holy Spirit also renews the function of our human spirit and restores the glory of God to our lives. By depending on Him first and foremost we allow Him to train us up in the way that we should go.

Colossians 1:26-27...the mystery that has been kept hidden for ages and generations, but is now disclosed to the saints. To them God has chosen to make known among the Gentiles the glorious riches of this mystery, which is Christ in you, the hope of glory.

The believer has gained intimacy as well as insight into the mind and heart of God. By having a renewed spirit we hear from heaven and are able to make right choices for body and soul. This is in contrast to how fallen man has lived his life, by the rule of his flesh; body and soul have inappropriately been ruling the roost. But now that we are alive in Christ we are being given a chance to conform to a new creation life and gain all the victory that is available by being one with Jesus in spirit.

Secondly, when we speak of new life, and new birth, we are talking about being hidden "in" God. He has supernaturally placed us within the Son that He loves and it is "in Him"; in His Spirit that we live, move and have our being.

John 17:20-22 "My prayer is not for them alone. I pray also for those who will believe in me through their message, 21 that all of them may be one, Father, just as you are in me and I am in you. May they also be in us so that the world may believe that you have sent me. 22 I have given them the glory that you gave me, that they may be one as we are one:

God supernaturally ushered us into the Kingdom, by supernaturally ushering us into the King.

If we remain in Jesus then we remain sealed within His life. He is our anchor offering a heavenly reality, even when a fallen world still wants to lay claim to us. Basically these two positional truths describe our union with Him:

- Christ "in us" empowers us to participate in His nature, character and righteous life.
- Being "in" Christ allows us to be in the world, but not of it. There is a great liberty in the environment of God's grace as well as freedom from the world, the flesh and the devil.

This place of sanctuary allows us to draw upon a true purpose and identity that is made in His image. All believers have been given this amazing privilege but to benefit from this gift requires that we remain attentive to where we dwell. Here is a story that brings this point to life.

Fresh Bread

As Ted walked down the sidewalk of his neighborhood, he caught the aroma of fresh bread baking. A neighbor, who happened to be a retired chef, had been baking one of his famous recipes, one which he received while in service to a very important family. The savory smell tantalized Ted's senses, and it became apparent that it was time to go and visit his neighbor and friend.

Just then, a stranger approached Ted and asked for directions, however the same fabulous whiff soon caught this stranger by surprise. He hesitated for a moment and then was moved to remark, "What a wonderful smell."

"You don't know the half of it," Ted said. "That is the aroma of hundreds of years of culinary perfection. A master chef retired after serving a very important European diplomat now graces our neighborhood with his culinary masterpieces."

The stranger replied, "I guess I'll have to stop by a bakery and buy myself a loaf."

Without hesitation Ted happily disagreed. "Oh there is "nothing found at a bakery that can compete with the quality of this chef's baking. The recipe is generations old and has been part of a secret recipe that has served kings." Another whiff of the baking bread causes Ted to expound a little more on the wonder of this masterpiece.

"A secret sourdough starter, hundreds of years old, is mixed into the finest whole grains. Every ingredient is screened for quality, using only organic flours, unrefined sea salt, and filtered spring water. Additional secret ingredients make the dough sticky, bubbly and pleasantly tart over a period of several hours."

The stranger then raised his eyebrows as he caught another generous whiff of the warm scent.

Ted continued; "As the warm dough ferments within the earthen crock it begins to rise with anticipation of its royal destiny," "The rich moist dough bulges from the crock and, like warm ironed linen, the aroma makes you long for home."

A slight wince revealed the stranger's new obsession. Maybe, just maybe, he would get a chance to partake of this potentially marvelous work of art. Yet for now all he could do was lean forward, almost on his tiptoes in an attempt to feed upon Ted's poetic sustenance.

"The dough is then kneaded with generous helpings of rich, silky flour. As it is pulled apart and cradled within fine bakery ware, each loaf again rises to the approval of the master chef."

The stranger is now bowing to the ache of a noisy stomach. A third deep breath makes the man dizzy with delight as Ted expounds upon the last part of the culinary journey.

"By the time the bread dough is proofed and marked for ascent, the Master Chef has readied a brick oven to receive his creation. As the loaves are gently placed within a heated bath of flames they undergo a remarkable moment of transformation.

The man swallowed hard and bowed to the approval of Ted's words. He then rocked back and forth in a state of culinary delirium longing to be satisfied with the golden brown aroma that wooed his senses.

Ted now spoke with a confident assurance that the master chef would soon receive his precious offspring; "the delicious loaves, naturally sour and naturally sweet, are nearly ready to debut. At the appointed time, a huge wooden paddle will gingerly swoop up two loafs at a time and place these golden brown fawns onto the cooling racks. As the warm bread is revealed there is a realization that its power over humanity is delightful."

By now, the stranger is salivating like Pavlov's dog.

Ted then lowered his voice for emphasis, as if honoring the loaves with human reverence. "They are then cradled in hand and delivered to the dining table where they receive generous portions of rich creamy butter. Each tear of the loaf releases the aroma and artistry of the master's touch. Superior flavor and texture give way to a full expression of human delight. In no time at all body and soul are satisfied, but only after the chewy, tangy, and fabulously fresh baked organic sourdough flavor rolls through your mouth!"

The stranger is now haggard. Ted had literally undone this man's will to go on without bread.

About this time the master chef's front door creaked opened and the chef was heard calling to his friend Ted; "Are you ready to come in?" Ted nodded with an agreeable wink and said, "I'll be right there." Without delay, he then puckishly said to the stranger, "well, I've got to go" and he exited the conversation with a mischievous glee in his step.

The stranger stared in disbelief. His shirt was now wrinkled where his sweaty hands had been seeking emotional support. His lips whimpered uncontrollably as he watched Ted gingerly enter the house of his friend and park himself in front of the dinning room window. A warm loaf of bread was set in front of Ted and he and his host began to talk, tear, and butter to their heart's delight.

"Is he looking at us?" the chef asked.

"Yep."

"Do you think he's satisfied with just the scent of fresh bread?"

"I don't think so. I laid it on pretty thick this time."

"I may be the master chef, but you have a knack for buttering up people!

Is he still looking?"

"Yes, and I think he's even crying."

"Oh, go let him in. Nobody can be satisfied by just talking about bread. Satisfaction comes in having your own loaf."

****

Genuine faith finds itself immersed in the life of Jesus. When that connection is made, He begins to share of Himself, and we become attached to His heart. Revelation is then born from an intimate friendship, rather than a best guess about what God is up to. You could say it's the difference between observation and actual participation in the life of Christ.

To be found in Jesus is to partake of the aroma of Christ, but also be granted access to the entire loaf.

<u>Application</u>
Jesus, I recognize that I died with You;
- **To serving a religious perspective that denies me all the benefits of You being in Me.**
- **To serving a religious perspective that denies me all the benefits of me being in You.**
- **To serving a faith, a ministry or an identity which is still outside of you.**

Jesus, I ask you to reveal to me the true authority which is found "in" You.

Because of our immersion into the life of the Savior, we learn to rely upon Him for everything. The body of Christ is then able to clearly see when there is a misuse of the Word, doctrine, authority and spiritual experience. Thus any potential "outside" threat, ("outside" referring to any concept that would rob us of our "in Him and Him in us" relationship) actually stands out like a sore thumb. In other words;

Being accustomed to the genuine helps us easily spot the counterfeit.

The Name of Jesus

There is also another aspect of authority that God has shared with us and it is found in His Name.

Colossians 3:17 And whatever you do, whether in word or deed, do it all in the name of the Lord Jesus, giving thanks to God the Father through him.

It is not merely reciting the name "Jesus" that is powerful, but rather it is the authority that is behind "The Name" and our position within it. Ultimately the nature and character of God rests on what Jesus came to accomplish for His people. The name "Jesus", or His original Hebrew name, "Yeshua" means; "Salvation."

John 17:11 I will remain in the world no longer, but they are still in the world, and I am coming to you. Holy Father, protect them by the power of your name—the name you gave me—so that they may be one as we are one.

The Father was pleased to give the Son a Name that is above every name and by having received salvation we too share in that Name. Think of it this way; when we proclaim His name we are letting both heaven and earth know that we are joint heirs with Christ and are declaring our Family Name!

Ephesians 3:14-15 For this reason I kneel before the Father, from whom his whole family in heaven and on earth derives its name.

From this family position, we can ask for the things that are found in God:

- We can ask for every advantage which is available to us in salvation.
- We can pray with effectiveness for ourselves and for others.
- We can declare freedom from bondage in physical, intellectual, and emotional ways.
- We can proclaim spiritual victory from the works of darkness.
- We can ask anything according to His will and He will give it to us.

John 16:23b-24 I tell you the truth, my Father will give you whatever you ask in my name. Until now you have not asked for anything in my name. Ask and you will receive, and your joy will be complete.

John 16:26-27 In that day you will ask in my name. I am not saying that I will ask the Father on your behalf. No, the Father himself loves you because you have loved me and have believed that I came from God.

When the Father gave us His Son He was setting precedence from that time forward; everything in heaven and earth would revolve around this one Person and the work that He has accomplished. The Name is perfect for declaring the will of God, but this does not mean it hasn't been misunderstood, misused or rendered powerless by religiosity.

Mark 13:5-6 Jesus said to them: "Watch out that no one deceives you. Many will come in my name, claiming, 'I am he,' and will deceive many.

The true power and authority of the Name of Jesus is maligned when we remain in charge of our own spiritual destiny. By having a natural mindset we inappropriately manipulate aspects of life and faith by placing hope in a name as if it were a magic word. Many have lost touch with the Author and Finisher of their faith for this very reason. As it became clear to me that I had made similar choices in my own walk with God I quickly repented and asked Him to uproot my improper beliefs and actions concerning Him and His Name.

Application
Jesus, I repent for my religious ideas about your Name. Forgive me for trying to "use it" as a tool or a weapon instead of understanding that I carry Your Family Name.
I recognize that I died with You to the following;
- **To being subject to the teachings of men, organizations, religion, a demonic realm or an angelic order that deliver improper beliefs about You and the authority of Your Name.**
- **To being subject to a spiritual realm that interrupts a pure exchange with You and the authority of Your Name.**

By virtue of my death, these improper covenants are broken.
I ask You to be the resurrection power that now saves me.

The natural authority of man still rules in earthly kingdoms, but the believer should trust that our God rules both heaven and earth. So we exercise authority by agreeing with His victory over the effects of the world and its many spiritual forces. Said in another way, we have gained authority by our agreement with all that God is and has accomplished.

2 Corinthians 3:17 Now the Lord is the Spirit, and where the Spirit of the Lord is, there is freedom. And we, who with unveiled faces all reflect the Lord's glory, are being transformed into his likeness with ever increasing glory, which comes from the Lord, who is the Spirit.

The advantages of the new creation over the first Adam are endless because God's Son now defines them from an eternal perspective. It is an authority that the Father was pleased to give Jesus, and it now becomes our source of authority as well.

Application
Jesus, I recognize I died with you to depending more on my fallen nature and Adamic authority than I do on my new authority in Christ.

We no longer have to succumb to the dictates of our fallen and fleshly nature, but we can now participate in a new life that trusts God and is empowered by His Spirit. However, whenever we attempt to handle our faith by the strength of our natural man it erodes our confidence in Christ and blinds us to His singular provision. These cause and effect dynamics are often created because we have chosen to yield ourselves over to the will of other men. The next chapter will speak to the root of this problem.

Linda's Comments

When something is alive and healthy it grows, so when our spiritual growth is stagnant it should be a warning sign that something is wrong. Our natural tendency is to add a little more religion, or a few more obligations to try and jumpstart our faith. The reality is that a believer who fails to thrive is one who did not receive a healthy biblical foundation. One of the most overlooked and important aspects of that foundation include the individual authority and purpose of each believer. Because of our death in Christ, the past has been wiped clean, not just from sin, but from the limitations of natural gifts, talents, and abilities. To be in Christ is to be a new creation that possesses His ability as well as His authority.

CHAPTER 5
Subjection and Submission

We don't give much thought to the subject, but we have often learned to maneuver through life and faith by participating in various stages of surrender. These actions can best be defined as "subjection and submission". On the one hand we can find ourselves subject to the things of the earth simply by being born into a fallen world. We didn't ask for this trouble, yet it came with the package.

"Subjection" can then be described as being under the power of something and is often the result of being held or forced against ones will.

On the other hand, we can also find ourselves subject to the things of this earth by our exercise of freewill. In this case:

"Submission" represents a willingness to give away aspects of ones authority in order to gain some perceived benefit.

If as believers we remain in either of these camps we can find ourselves pressed by a lesser quality of life and frequently "under" the control of a lesser god. Let's allude to one of Paul's statements to add some perspective;

Romans 6:16a Don't you know that when you offer yourselves to someone as obedient slaves, you are slaves of the one you obey—

It is almost as if Paul is saying that we have a "choice"; we can either remain a free people or we can choose to be subject to other agendas. Yet if a wrong choice commences a loss of sovereignty often sets us under the control of a person, an organization, a philosophy, an unjust law or even a spiritual power. Poor choices will then effect how we respond in body, soul and spirit, mind, will, emotions, moral conscience, conscious and subconscious thought, intimacy, sexuality, authority, identity, Christianity, family, communication, intellect, and gender. Now that is quite a list of potential "cause and effect" type problems. But let me first point out that this is not where we started in Christ.

Remember when you were just saved how free you felt? Every baby Christian starts their Christian walk with a clean slate. The things that once owned them in body, soul and spirit were severed. In fact the Word reinforces this point of liberty by calling the believer a "new creation"; one that is not "subject" to the old creation.

2 Corinthians 5:17 (NKJV) Therefore, if anyone is in Christ, he is a new creation; old things have passed away; behold, all things have become new.

The Strongs (G2537) concordance calls this being; "of a new kind, unprecedented, novel, uncommon, unheard of." Basically we have been set free of the "old man" and have been deemed new. This also coincides with Jesus having gone before us; He is called, "the first born Son from among the dead" (Colossians 1:18).

God supernaturally invites us to be a part of His death, burial and resurrection and this clears away the clutter.

So in simple terms, every believer starts out unhindered and free of the burdens of a fallen world. Again, Paul has something to say on this foundational matter;

1Cor 3:11-13 For no one can lay any foundation other than the one already laid, which is Jesus Christ. If any man builds on this foundation using gold, silver, costly stones, wood, hay or straw, his work will be shown for what it is, because the Day will bring it to light. It will be revealed with fire, and the fire will test the quality of each man's work.

Keep in mind that we who are in Christ base our safety and assurances on being a part of the foundation. It is from this place of security that we learn to depend on God for everything. We really have no need to go beyond these safe borders because the foundation offers us great liberty. Yet if our faith decides to add or subtract from God's complete provision, we then weaken our Christian stance and reengage the world on its own terms. In this manner we have been know to return to "life as usual" and subject ourselves to past ownership. Any old pattern of thought or action as well as any new flirtation with the world can cause us to experience a significant loss of Christian identity and authority.

Kingdom of Dominance

Before the fall man kept his focus on God and prospered in his attempts to steward creation. However after the fall, man became quite self-centered. As he looked upon his own form and function, he had no other choice but to make life's journey all about himself. Hence his self centered approach made him a negative force to be reckoned with; God's commission to take dominion was replaced with a drive to simply dominate. Jesus also gives us a glimpse of this fallen imbalance of power:

Mark 10:42-44 Jesus called them together and said, "You know that those who are regarded as rulers of the Gentiles lord it over them, and their high officials exercise authority over them. 43Not so with you. Instead, whoever wants to become great among you must be your servant, 44and whoever wants to be first must be slave of all.

This infection within humanity was initially inspired by the Devil's own search for greatness.

Isaiah 14:13-14 You said in your heart, "I will ascend to the heavens; I will raise my throne above the stars of God; I will sit enthroned on the mount of assembly, on the utmost heights of Mount Zaphon. 14 I will ascend above the tops of the clouds; I will make myself like the Most High."

The Devil's attempt to become equal with God was also a self centered exploit. His narcissistic attitude made him believe that he was the most likely candidate for advancement in heaven. Of course his reckless coup failed, and he found himself expelled from heaven, yet still motivated to try and gain recognition.

As Adam and Eve embraced the Tree of the knowledge of good and evil they were saying good-bye to paradise, but they were also saying hello to the Devil's world view. Basically as they accepted the Devils sales pitch they came "under" his dominance and control and were prompted to adopt his same narcissistic ways. This of course means that men have been conditioned to strive for higher ground in life as well as in relationships. Subsequently there is no equality among men, but rather a drive to dominate others as a means of self-preservation and self-promotion. So, whenever a worldly agenda is unleashed upon us it inappropriately presses us to conform and submit to its physical, intellectual, emotional, and spiritual demands, and we often comply. That place of improper submission is a stronghold that denies us fullness in Christ.

Dominion Renewed

Now I can say with assurance that no Christian has escaped rubbing shoulders with the world but continuing to trust in the Cross of Christ offers us a reprieve from its clutches. Jesus remains exalted above all mankind's fallen antics and He is waiting for us to take our rightful place of authority in Him.

Ephesians 2:6-7 And God raised us up with Christ and seated us with him in the heavenly realms in Christ Jesus, 7 in order that in the coming ages he might show the incomparable riches of his grace, expressed in his kindness to us in Christ Jesus.

Seated with Christ means two things; it means we have ceased from our own works, since Jesus has offered us a full and rich alternative to mankind's dominion. Secondly it means that we have gained a spiritual authority in Christ that is raised above the dictates of fallen creation. For this reason the spiritual new creation that defines us in Christ has a say over this once dominant world. We literally can look down from above and hold on to a perspective that the kingdoms of this world are under our feet.

Please let this sink in. We have authority that is greater than Adam's. Adam had fleshly authority and he gave it away to the Devil. But we have been brought into Christ, and have gained spiritual authority which is raised above anything that the world tries to throw at us. When we were given this position in Jesus it allowed us to participate in every victory He has delivered. We don't have to be under anything that inappropriately seeks to own or control us.

Galatians 5:1 It is for freedom that Christ has set us free. Stand firm, then, and do not let yourselves be burdened again by a yoke of slavery.

Now that should explain how we live our lives moving forward, but what do we do with past choices that currently own us? For the record we can't go back and relive yesterday, but we can certainly be free of its lingering influence. Sadly many believers live their lives as if the past still dictates their way. They made poor choices years ago and those contracts are still holding them captive to men, organizations, and a demonic; but in Christ we can sever these bad choices.

Take any issue (One at a time of course) where you believe that the world still owns you and holds you captive. By agreeing with Jesus at the Cross, He can separate you from any improper influence known to Adam.

Application
Jesus, I repent for once again entangling myself in the world with its good and evil agendas. I repent for choosing natural authority over what you offer me.
I recognize I died with you;
- **To being subject or improperly submissive to _____. (Name an activity or bondage.)**
- **To being subject or improperly submissive to men and organizations that promote this same form of bondage. (Name them)**
- **To being subject to a spiritual realm that supports these issues.**

By virtue of my death, burial and resurrection with you, these improper covenants are broken.
I ask You to be the resurrection power that now saves me.

I'm sure that initially you can think of a number of issues that need to be looked at, but for a thorough house cleaning consider the following:

A Christian is the temple of God, made new and filled with the Holy Spirit. As believers we should take every opportunity to "let Jesus out". However due to our propensity to act natural it would be wise to be suspect of anything trying to "get in".

These issues of subjection and submission also have a significant effect on faith.

Additions to Faith
Colossians 2:20-23 Since you died with Christ to the elemental spiritual forces of this world, why, as though you still belonged to the world, do you submit to its rules:

21 "Do not handle! Do not taste! Do not touch!"? 22 These rules, which have to do with things that are all destined to perish with use, are based on merely human commands and teachings. 23 Such regulations indeed have an appearance of wisdom, with their self-imposed worship, their false humility and their harsh treatment of the body, but they lack any value in restraining sensual indulgence.

When our faith is compromised by natural thinking and natural authority we start adding good and evil concepts to it. These are nothing more than religious notions born out of man's attempts to make Christianity work. When this happens we end up leaving a simple salvation message and add multiple layers of complexity to our walk. Here's my theory:

The simplest gospel is the one God first gave.

Now keep in mind that heaven is still responding to our authority in Christ. If a person decides that standing on one's head is the way to God, then heaven will actually honor this person's faith.

"Let us stand on our heads and pray"

Faith is the key; if we want to define the Christian life with added obligation then those additions to faith will now become a required step. God didn't ask it of us; however we are the ones choosing to be bound in this way. An interesting example of added compulsion can be found in 1 Samuel 8: 4-18 (my paraphrase).

The elders of Israel come before Samuel the Prophet and say they want to have a king to lead them, much like other nations have. Samuel being disturbed by their request sought God on the matter. God says to give the people what they want, but also warn them that they are asking for unnecessary servitude and oppression in order to appease this fleshly urge for a human king.

Based on similar dynamics we may be adding unhealthy subjection and submission issues to our walk in order to satisfy a human itch. Some of these choices may seem insignificant at the time, yet they can also be the root cause of a life time of added detours and religious mistakes.

These issues are also what divide the Church. While some rest in God and trust in a simple message, others are driven to conform to any number of rules, regulations, and rituals and often expect others to do the same. These obligations occupy our time and attention and deny us freedom and maturity in Christ.

Additions to faith are also a spiritually charged matter. Because we are looking to connect with a spiritual God we anticipate that spiritual reward and interaction should follow. However, if our natural man continues to add to the foundation, religious commands, obligations, and commitments begin to invite counterfeit powers to back up our belief system. What we have created is a two part stronghold. Our first mistake was becoming a child of religion and the second was becoming a slave to its gods.

These two points lead us on a dysfunctional journey that doesn't allow us to find rest. Subsequently once this path is adopted we push onward and upward collecting more and more religious debris with the hopes that one day our subservience will finally reward us. However our religious devotion has no choice but to eventually fail.

If we come to the conclusion that we can no longer support religious principles, then we should be willing to take these bad contracts to the Cross. In so doing we are actually fulfilling a scriptural principle spoken to us by Paul the Apostle.

2 Corinthians 13:5 Examine yourselves to see whether you are in the faith; test yourselves. Do you not realize that Christ Jesus is in you—unless, of course, you fail the test?

Testing the quality of our faith is as simple as letting God take our doctrines, our rituals, our attempts at ministry and spiritual source of power into death with Him. In so doing we can be restored to a simple faith and a true ministry of the Spirit.

Application
Jesus, I recognize that I died with You;
- **To being subject to a religious principle (name one) that has nothing to do with You.**
- **To being subject to any religion promoting a physical, intellectual, emotional and spiritual obligation that you do not endorse.**
- **To being subject to others that support the same.**

By virtue of my death, these improper covenants are broken.
I ask You to be the resurrection power that now saves me.

Linda's Comments

Just as with everything else in the Kingdom of God, submission becomes simple when it is found in Christ. However, when people improperly submit to a leader based on religion that leader feels obligated to try and save them. This is a heavier burden than any one man or woman should carry.

After I came to understand my death with Christ, I realized that I had actually been violating the Church with my religious expectations and I needed to repent for treating church members like children. I had actually been usurping their authority in Christ. When I took this matter to the Cross I found freedom from an improper obligation to be their surrogate parent and in turn they gained a necessary freedom from me. Challenging the validity of any past religious action or contract is essential if we intend on having a healthy faith and church experience.

CHAPTER 6
Being the Church

The One New Man

As your mind is renewed to the fullness that is available in Jesus, a revelation unfolds revealing an assembly of people all fitted and joined together as a single new man. What a marvelous sight! It's as if a body were being knitted together right before your very eyes. With delicate woven precision each individual part is being gathered together with a single strand of light. That thread is "truth" and it now holds you within a living, breathing organism.

Millions of unified cells stand poised on the edge of eternity united by a heavenly call. It is at that very moment that the Father of lights enters the heart of this new creation and a hush ensues as the Eternal King begins to speak; "I love you --- I am well pleased with you, and I honor you this day"

The commanding power of the Maker's voice echoes with waves of delight even reverberating to the four corners of heaven. His sweet inviting words kiss the face of every cell and they each blush with delight. The person to your left glances at you and nods, as if to confirm the wonder of being fully known; while the one on your right can do nothing more than giggle.

This "new man" is Jesus and it is the Father affectionately speaking to His Son. As you ponder the significance of this event, for the first time in your life you understand being made one with the Creator. All these cells are gathered together within this One New Creation and there is a sense of genuine connection which can only be described as "perfect fellowship".

From this place of grace you begin to understand the benefits of really belonging to God. He is calling you to not only be a part of the whole, but also share in the knowledge of the One. For no one can say that they have seen Jesus from your vantage point, and it is this revelation that makes your service unique and essential.

Personal pride finds no footing, because you are more interested in hearing from each cell; "Tell me what you know about Jesus. Please, don't hold anything back; I've got to know all about Him from where you stand!"

As you rest in the glow of His Glory you are filled with the splendor and the aroma of His eternal grace, you come to realize that the next moment in God's Son will be as great and glorious as the last!

A Spiritual Body

Because we are in Christ, God's kingdom is available to us without limit and we gain a whole new perspective on life. A life that was once moved by fallen principles or a fallen nature can now be moved by the power of God's Holy Spirit. This transition offers us new purpose and identity. By handing over the reigns of our heart, God is able to provide us with a true heavenly call; one that is formed and fitted within eternity.

Now that's an interesting way to see life, "eternally". When the believer adopts an eternal perspective it's because they finally came in contact with an eternal God. For this reason we can realistically conclude that the Christian life isn't "all about us".

This same assertion can be made when looking at the Church. Two thousand years ago Jesus declared;

Matthew 16:18b I will build my church, and the gates of Hades will not overcome it.

In that moment of time Jesus was revealing that He had plans for a Church body that was made in His image. Soon after He spoke these words He went to the cross, died, was buried and then rose again. By these actions He was showing us that the way in which the Church would be born again was through a spiritual means. His death, burial and resurrection became the place that all believers were gathered together in Him.

2 Corinthians 5:14-15 For Christ's love compels us, because we are convinced that one died for all, and therefore all died. 15And he died for all, that those who live should no longer live for themselves but for him who died for them and was raised again.

This describes the essential nature of God's universal Church and represents the place in which all believers, as well as all generations, find proper title and unity. This is the Church that we speak of; it is a spiritual body of believers that have found their place in the life and purposes of God. Somewhere beyond any human construct there is a people that are made complete by God's power to save and are then commissioned to shine forth His light. They worship and serve the Creator who makes fellowship a celebration and unity a birthright. Such a Church body radiates His presence even when the smallest number of believers come together declaring His Name.

Matthew 18:20 For where two or three gather in my name, there am I with them."

A definition for "the Church" should be just that simple and uncomplicated. When we begin with all that Jesus is and has done, the Church finds itself complete and undivided. Consider the scope of the Gospel's claim to an undivided people.

- *1 Corinthians 10:17 ...Because there is one loaf, we, who are many, are one body, for we all partake of the one loaf.*
- *Ephesians 1:10 ... to bring all things in heaven and on earth together under one head, even Christ.*
- *Ephesians 3:6 This mystery is that through the gospel the Gentiles are heirs together with Israel, members together of one body.*
- *Ephesians 4:4-6 There is one body and one Spirit--just as you were called to one hope when you were called--one Lord, one faith, one baptism; one God and Father of all, who is over all and through all and in all.*

This single Savior is our Life and Hope. He is the sole interpreter of all that comes from above and His preeminence makes a healthy Church possible.

The Measure of a Cell

What we are talking about is a vibrant organic expression of Church life, one that is properly connected to its Head and moves to the beat of God's heart; a heart that is more interested in relationship rather than religion. As we accept our place in this Eternal Body we begin to realize that there is a functional place of assignment for each of us.

An assignment can best be described as an opportunity to share with others some aspect of the free gift of God. As He makes Himself known to us or shows us a particular kindness it inspires us to offer others a similar gift. Such a commission may serve the basic needs of humanity or it can represent a spiritual gift that edifies the whole Body.

Ephesians 4:16 NKJV From whom the whole body fitly joined together and compacted by that which every joint supplieth, according to the effectual working in the measure of every part, maketh increase of the body unto the edifying of itself in love.

Assignment orchestrated by God also includes a certain sphere of influence. The word "measure" as it is used above, is describing not only our place of authority, but also the extent of our reach. The Greek word for "measure" here is "metron" and denotes a vessel for receiving and determining the quantity of things; it is a parameter or a portion measured to us. So as we receive our marching orders from God, we also look for Him to decide who and what is to be touched by our actions.

Ephesians 2:21-22 In him the whole building is joined together and rises to become a holy temple in the Lord. 22 And in him you too are being built together to become a dwelling in which God lives by his Spirit.

Some are called to teach; some are called to bring forth a word, some offer worship and service; while still others minister aspects of God's favor. Yet in each case we look for the true stature of Christ to be revealed.

Ephesians 4:7a, 15 But to each one of us grace has been given as Christ apportioned it……
15 Instead, speaking the truth in love, we will in all things grow up into him who is the Head, that is, Christ.

If a true Gospel flows through our veins then Jesus brings us together to carry out His eternal purpose. Basically we each have a calling given to us by God and this allows us to minister to the lives of others while in union and in harmony with our Savior. Yet not everyone is inspired or motivated to take their proper place in the kingdom.

Another Church

So if we have authority, position, assignment, unity and equality in Jesus; what is stifling us in our quest to glorify Him?
The most likely answer is; we have decided to take charge and build the church as "we think" best. However when viewing the Church through natural eyes we will start to cater to a different agenda in the faith. This environment promotes fleshly obligation and sets goals that are temporal and earthly; they certainly don't have any eternal significance or value. On that note I refer back to one of Paul's insightful statements;

***Romans 8: 5-6** Those who live according to the flesh have their minds set on what the flesh desires; but those who live in accordance with the Spirit have their minds set on what the Spirit desires. 6 The mind governed by the flesh is death, but the mind governed by the Spirit is life and peace.*

Paul is speaking to all of us in one way or another. For me, having once been committed to a zealous group of believers meant that I had invited all sorts of added obligations into my faith. As I yielded to their way of thinking I naturally began to reflect their character and the "spirit" that moved them. This is how a believer gets pulled out of heaven and is made a slave to religious principles. Whenever we lose our anchor in Christ we will automatically place too much emphasis on our flesh in an attempt to succeed. We will also want to compare ourselves to men rather than Christ.

Let me emphasize this point: if we use our minds, hands and feet to glorify religious interests we can find ourselves managed, molded, corralled, and subservient to the dictates of a counterfeit work. In such an environment, how we respond to leadership changes significantly.

Now, before we look at any potential problems apparent in serving religious leadership let's first present a healthy picture of God's government.

God's Government

Church government or the five-fold ministry represents the role of the apostle, prophet, evangelist, pastor and teacher. God initially commissioned these governmental roles in order to bring stability and maturity to the Body of Christ.

***Ephesians 4:10-13** He who descended is the very one who ascended higher than all the heavens, in order to fill the whole universe. It was he who gave some to be apostles, some to be prophets, some to be evangelists, and some to be pastors and teachers to prepare God's people for works of service, so that the body of Christ may be built up until we all reach unity in the faith and in the knowledge of the Son of God and become mature, attaining to the whole measure of the fullness of Christ.*

When Jesus chose these ministers of the Gospel He did so with the intention they would be an extension of His will; or maybe better

said an extension of His own ministry. Consider what the Word has to say about Jesus being the fulfillment of His government.
- **Apostle**-----Heb. 3:1 - Jesus is the apostle and high priest of our confession.
- **Prophet**--Rev. 19:10 -The testimony of Jesus is the spirit of prophecy."
- **Evangelist**-Luke 4:18-Jesus was anointed to preach good news to the poor.
- **Pastor** --Heb. 13:21 - Jesus is the great Shepherd of the sheep.
- **Teacher**-Matt. 23:10- Jesus is our teacher.

The five-fold ministry is very much alive today, but it is only found in Christ.
- As Jesus is lifted up as the Apostle and High Priest, He gives assignment to His servants providing foundational truth and leadership.
- When Jesus the Prophet speaks, those who prophecy reveal the very heart and mind of God.
- When Jesus reveals Himself as the Good News, we see the evangelist bring in converts.
- When Jesus Shepherds His people, we see the pastor nurturing and encouraging the Church to mature and become fruitful.
- When Jesus teaches, those who educate reveal a clear and simple truth that sets people free.

We can confidently say that without Jesus being our source there is no gifting, calling, anointing, or government. Without Him, the Church lacks meaningful direction and effective leadership.

When the Leader Has Two Masters
Hebrews 13:7 Remember your leaders, who spoke the word of God to you. Consider the outcome of their way of life and imitate their faith.

I believe in God's government. The five fold ministry is important to us in our walk with God. We need leaders to provide genuine insights into the kingdom and the life of Jesus. Though a Christian minister is called by God to carry a governmental role and retain a metron of godly influence, they too can find themselves distracted by a religious mindset. Basically, when a minister is thinking naturally about the kingdom he is thinking religiously. Mind you, we are not saying that leadership isn't going to minister to the natural needs of people; however a leader's work is of its greatest value when he is able to point them in the direction of Christ.

For this reason we cannot compare God's government to what we are accustomed to in the world. Elected officials, judges, and all other authority figures that serve the earth and its world system can't do things God's way. However the apostle, prophet, evangelist, pastor or teacher would do well to first seek the Spirit of God for solutions rather than follow natural inclinations. In other words learn and then teach what is possible by the power of our spiritual God and Savior.

So what is the result if we embrace natural man's take on God and His kingdom?

Fallen Adamic authority tends to dominate, which equates to one man ruling over another. A congregation can then inappropriately find itself obligated to submit and conform to the wishes of that fleshly leader rather than to the will of God. Hence when Christian leadership becomes religious, answers regarding life and faith become a reflection of a singular man's brand of wisdom if not simply his own brand of religion. Jesus helps us gain more insight on this subject by saying:

Matthew 15:8-9 This people honors me with their lips, but their heart is far away from me. But in vain do they worship me, teaching as doctrines the precepts of men.

A "precept" is a rule or principle that imposes a standard of action or conduct upon us. This causes a congregation to conform to an agenda that appears successful based on human standards but falls short of ever gaining a renewed heart and mind. Maybe I should say it like this; if we embrace a religious leader then on a good day we are actually only learning about their relationship with God rather than being able to cultivate our own. Human ingenuity often pulls ministry out of heavenly realms and robs the Church of its true Spirit led victory and calling.

So, what is the proper role of leadership? Look no further then

Eph. 4:11-13: To equip his (God's) people for works of service, so that the body of Christ may be built up until we all reach unity in the faith and in the knowledge of the Son of God and become mature, attaining to the whole measure of the fullness of Christ.

Hopefully you can see the importance of setting aside a natural way of defining ministry and the minister. We don't deny men a say in our lives, but neither should we allow them to have inappropriate influence in our walk with God. Has the Church as a whole obtained its true stature and gained fullness apart from such improper dominance? I'm sorry to say our efforts have been in vain. It is not the genuine commission or message that is suspect; it is only that which has been incrementally added to the foundation that creates confusion and religious bondage. This is also a significant factor in explaining why there is a rise in Church discontentment, lethargy and apathy. Unless the people are allowed to be an active participant in the family of God they die on the vine.

Application
Jesus, I repent for glorifying my own religious views and that of others over and above you and your Holy Spirits provision.
I recognize that I died with You;
- **To inappropriately being subject to apostles, prophets, evangelists, pastors or teachers that retain a physical or natural title and ministry rather than one set in place by your Spirit.**
- **To being obligated to conform to their religious ways in body, soul and spirit when it deviates from your foundation of Spirit and truth.**
- **To being subject to my own or to other's religious perceptions of what authority, service and submission should look and act like.**
- **To improperly owning Your people with my own faulty religion and attempts at fleshly leadership.**
- **To being subject to a spiritual realm that support all these issues.**

By virtue of my death, these improper covenants are broken.
I ask You to be the resurrection power that now saves me and saves others from me.

Linda's Comments
In the Kingdom of God the ground is level at the foot of the Cross. No one is exalted but Jesus; the rest of us are brothers and sisters each with differing assignments from the Father. One assignment is no greater than the other; each of us is simply given the

opportunity to obey God and depend on the Holy Spirit to complete the task. In Christ there is perfect honor for each believer.

Now that my own religious perspective of being a leader is gone, I can be known for who I really am; I'm a sister in Christ who walks beside other brothers and sisters. Because true submission is for everyone, I am as delighted to submit to the Jesus in my brothers and sisters as they are now free to submit to the Jesus in me.

When the Congregation Has Two Masters

Though the need for leadership to reclaim their proper function in Christ is of profound importance, it has not been the only barrier to a healthy Church. As it happens, a religious church doesn't expect equality in Christ; instead it wants to be held within a comfort zone. Basically our human nature or our Adamic nature wants prescribed boundaries set for it where someone else is made responsible for our growth. We also want someone to tell us how to be "good" so that we can remain in favor and avoid chastisement. For this reason we give men honorary title and unlimited reach into our lives. Yet Jesus had something to say on this matter.

Matthew 23:8-11 "But you are not to be called 'Rabbi,' for you have one Teacher, and you are all brothers. 9 And do not call anyone on earth 'father,' for you have one Father, and he is in heaven. 10 Nor are you to be called instructors, for you have one Instructor, the Messiah. 11 The greatest among you will be your servant.

I like how Philips translation puts these verses:

Don't you ever be called 'rabbi'—you have only one teacher, and all of you are brothers. And don't call any human being 'father'—for you have one Father and he is in Heaven. And you must not let people call you 'leaders'—you have only one leader, Christ! The only 'superior' among you is the one who serves the others.

This is an example of finding comfort in the familiar, which often parallels some of our family dynamics. Consider how family gets pulled into the picture when we become religious.

Father

Since the Church is often viewed as "a godly family" people will automatically reflect the level of health they once knew while in the home. However years of conditioning usually allows unresolved issues to fester. Successes and failures once found in conjunction with father, mother, brothers, and sisters, are reinstated, and the proverbial pecking order is revived.

This becomes a loaded weapon that no leader or congregation is equipped to handle. Suddenly, the leader ceases to be viewed as a brother or sister in Christ, equal in authority and purpose; instead they are viewed as a surrogate parent catering to the needs of perpetual children. Under such conditions personal interaction with God is replaced with a dependency on leadership. The result is a significant diminishing of each believer's authority and their ability to trust in God.

This is dangerous to the health and safety of the body of Christ; there are aspects of our lives that should naturally be off limits to leadership. They don't necessarily belong in the management of our homes, how we dress, where we work or who we should marry. But if we "hand over" those areas of our lives we will become subject to their personal good and evil standards. In contrast if you teach a believer the Cross and their authority in Christ you raise up a mature son or daughter free of distraction. This allows the Heavenly Father to take His rightful place on the throne of their hearts and lead them into a righteous and productive life.

Let's look again at *Matthew 23:9*;

"And do not call anyone on earth 'father,' for you have one Father, and he is in heaven,"

This word in the Greek is pathvr (Pater) it emphasizes the especially close and intimate relationship man has with God. It also speaks of "Pater" as being an originator, as well as the author of a family or society. "Pater" is one who infuses His Spirit into others, who actuates and governs their minds.

In other words, God is our "source".

"Do not call anyone on earth your (source) for you have one (source), and He is in heaven."

Mother

Once we set the stage by adopting a religious father a motherly role can also come into play. Usually a pastor's wife or some other mature woman will step into a nurturing position. If she embraces the same parental pattern then she draws inspiration from her humanity rather then from Christ. In this manner she may offer examples of love and affection which are common maternal traits, but they become a substitute for God's own ability to nurture us by His Spirit.

In truth the parental role doesn't belong in the Church. A man or woman's positive attributes and affirmations may be a good standard in the home, yet it still remains an imperfect standard of what we should be looking for from God.

One other thing worth mentioning on this subject: I don't know about you, but I found it difficult at times to listen to a parent's counsel and respond to them with glad enthusiasm. Certainly I would do what they say, but truthfully my heart wasn't always ready to accept their instruction. Under the veil of domestic roles a designated church parent may also find difficulty in getting through to a congregation that is entrenched in adolescent rebellion. In other words there is little response to the message entering the heart since it only serves to engage the flesh.

Another dynamic that comes into play with the child/parent role, is that we lose our ability to follow the Holy Spirit's leading. This is simply due to an unspoken obligation to wait for permission and approval from the proverbial parent or guardian's direction. Yet this becomes a point of reckless submission. Paul addresses this matter in the following way;

1 Timothy 4:1-2 But the Spirit explicitly says that in later times some will fall away from the faith, paying attention to deceitful spirits and doctrines of demons, by means of the hypocrisy of liars seared in their own conscience as with a branding iron,

Liars seared in their conscience?

When we hear this statement we don't think it could possibly have anything to do with our connection to the Church. Instead we dismiss this as being the work of evil men who are set on carrying out evil plans. Yet Paul in his day was speaking of men that served the law. In essence they were teaching a religion that says God's favor only comes about through fleshly good works. Under such conditioning religion often reinforces concepts such as "do not handle, do not taste and do not touch; and just as compulsory "do" handle, "do" taste and "do" touch. Yet even in our best attempts to be like Jesus, mimicking Him falls short of actually being truly united with Him. Subsequently if anyone chooses to participate in the religious box then they choose to live by the rules of that box. Under such rule our conscience gets "branded" (seared) with an obligation to perform and conform to a bogus code of ethics.

This is how Christian cults come about. They may start off serving sound doctrine and a trust in the Holy Spirit's leading, yet by adding ritual and rhetoric to the program greater degrees of subservience to mankind's ways develop. This dynamic can unfold in any size group, from a Mega church to a home group.

<u>**Application**</u>
Jesus, I recognize that I died with You;
- **To being subject to others that have been given the power to falsely mediate in my relationship with You. (name them)**
- **To being subject to these people and ministers having power to turn on or turn off my relationship with You.**
- **To being subject to a false example of the family of God that has been imposed upon my Christian walk by a religious father, mother and substitute savior roles.**
- **To being improperly subject to the natural man's domestic authority while in the Church and his or her example of love, joy, peace, patience, kindness, gentleness and self control. Name some other qualities.**
- **To being subject to teachings and human commands that have the appearance of wisdom, with self-imposed worship, false humility and harsh treatment of the body, but lack any value in restraining "mine or anyone else's" sensual indulgence.**
- **To being subject to men, organizations, denominations, a demonic realm or an angelic order that deny me access to You as the One True God and Savior.**
- **To being subject to a spiritual realm that support these same issues.**

By virtue of my death, these improper covenants are broken.
I ask You to be the resurrection power that now saves me.

Linda's Comments

Since the fall the strongest drive in natural man is self preservation. We will do just about anything to keep ourselves alive, well, and happy, but most of all safe.

For most of us the first place we felt safe was in our parent's arms. We were cared for, fed, nurtured, clothed and protected. For this reason we will often spend a lifetime trying to find that same level of security. Our most "natural" tendency is to assign someone that honorary role in our lives and we willingly abdicate our rights to anyone who we think can provide these things. However, when we do this we submit to the weaknesses as well as the strengths of the person we have chosen. Even though it may seem like a good idea, God never intended His leaders to take this role in His people's lives. Christ came and died so that every believer could have the Holy Spirit and each could have an intimate relationship with the Father.

We will fail to see the equality that we long for in Christ if we continue to give our authority away to other men and women. When we inappropriately elevate them above ourselves, the proper role of leadership gets taken out of context and blown up to become something it was never intended to be.

Coming Free of the Confusion

Just for effect, consider the following: if someone was to start carrying around a ten pound weight; then their posture would change, their gate would be altered and exhaustion would eventually settle in. It is also likely that their attitudes would change as they yielded to the added physical burden. Religion has a similar effect; a religious concept is not just a principle that occupies the mind, instead it lays hold of our whole person and changes how we respond in physical, intellectual, emotional and spiritual ways.

Having decided to carry this weight by choice it is likely we will not complain at first; instead we would probably believe that the added obligation is just part of the way God works. We might even say; "it is required of us" if we really want all of God. In essence we have just made an initial contract that we are now obligated to uphold. But of course one bad contract leads to even heavier burdens. Hundreds of small choices can add up to one very large diversion to our faith.

Whenever we find ourselves unsettled or outside God's place of rest it is a good bet that a bad contract or erroneous agreement is the root cause. Basically a lack of peace suggests that we are already owned in some way by the improper mediation of men, organizations, religion, or even a demonic realm.

1 Timothy 2:5;For there is one God and one mediator between God and mankind, the man Christ Jesus,

A mediator stands between two parties, so when we speak of faith towards God how many mediators are supposed to stand between us and the Father? It is at this moment we need Jesus to bring order out of the chaos and speak to us about whatever is keeping us apart.

His Voice
John 10:27 My sheep listen to my voice; I know them, and they follow me.

We shouldn't expect the voice of God to be a verbal narrative, though there are exceptions to the rule. His simplest voice is a prompting within our hearts which nudges us to consider; consider His ways or consider what is before us. The response I personally get from the Holy Spirit includes an initial thought or image that reminds me of a person, event or some ordeal that is at the root of my dysfunction. This lets me know that I have likely made a questionable choice in the past that improperly links me with that entity. In other words I'm under its power and subject to its influence in such a way that it hinders and changes how I currently respond in life and faith. Linda offers an interesting take on this very subject:

> Once when I was counseling a woman I was surprised to hear that she had never had the sense that God had spoken to her even though she had been a believer for over 15 years. I told her that it was her birthright in Christ to know His voice (John 10:27). I then asked her, "Did you give away your right to hear God? Have you been counting on someone else to hear God for you?"
> Later that evening as I thought back over our conversation I asked God, "Have I ever done the same thing?" Immediately a memory flashed in my mind from when I was 12 years old. I was raised in a non Christian home and had no real background in spiritual things; except that I knew God was good and the

devil was bad. I had just received Christ a week earlier at a vacation bible school and had been reading the little bible that they had given me like a starving person finally getting to eat. I had also been listening to preachers on my little transistor radio. One of them preached for a while and then said that if people would send in a love offering he would go before God and get a "word" for them. I was so excited that I ran to my bedroom and grabbed the box that held my money. I got 50 cents a week allowance and had saved $11.70; so I put the money in an envelope and mailed it to him.

God clearly brought this memory to mind because as a baby Christian I didn't know that it was possible to personally know His voice, so I assumed that a preacher must be the one to do it for me.

God showed me that at the very beginning of my faith I naively gave away my birthright and even paid the man to take it. A quick prayer cleared the slate of any lingering hindrance to my relationship and communication with Jesus.

This offers us insights into how an innocent exchange can stifle a healthy relationship with God. It not only created an improper subjection to a man, but also added a dubious spiritual link.

The Spirit without the Word

Basically when we go looking for our own divine connections we get a wrong number. In such instances men are more than willing to offer up advice and other powers are more than willing to tickle our ears, entertain our senses and distract us from God's true call and purpose. In fact religion always comes packed with all sorts of wonderful warm fuzzy feelings that validate a counterfeit message.

Timothy 4:1 The Spirit clearly says that in later times some will abandon the faith and follow deceiving spirits and things taught by demons.

The King James Version calls these spirits "seducing spirits"; they seek to touch man's senses in ways that place too much importance on natural feelings and desires; let me explain.

The reason for much of our spiritual blindness has to do with the original fall. Having once been clothed by God's glory, the loss of that radiance makes man seek for another source of spiritual support. When believers become religious they are trying to regain a covering even though they have already been made complete and covered in Christ. Rather than depending on the glory of God that abides within them they seek to affirm their flesh and gain validation by the senses. By bringing emphasis to our flesh we mistakenly believe that our senses will never lie to us; I feel good therefore my spiritual encounter must be real and from God! In those moments of delusion the one true Savior does try to curb the madness of His child's wants. However our familiarity and dependence on our feelings often speaks louder than the inner counsel of the Holy Spirit. Here is a scenario that happens more often than we would like to admit.

> "God I see that you favor Jane with supernatural experiences and I want to know that I am just as important to you as she is".
> *I am favoring you, that is why I'm not allowing you to have that counterfeit experience.*
> But God I really, really want that power and ability!
> *No my child that is not for you.*
> Certainly a demon must be trying to deny me a good spiritual gift ---- I rebuke you in the name of Jesus.
> *Child it's Me; and I am trying to save you from the heartache and slavery associated with a seducing spirit and a false religion.*
> That's it I am going to press in and win this battle until I get what I want!
> *OK my child - I will remove my hedge of protection because you remain so insistent.*

How do we avoid similar spiritual delusions?
When it comes to any religious encounter that offers enhanced natural or spiritual abilities, the Word says we should test the Spirits to see if they are of God.

1 John 4:1 Dear friends, do not believe every spirit, but test the spirits to see whether they are from God, because many false prophets have gone out into the world. 2 This is how you can recognize the Spirit of God: Every spirit that acknowledges that Jesus Christ has come in the flesh is from God, 3 but every spirit that does not acknowledge Jesus is not from God.

In this passage John was not suggesting that we spend our time talking to demons. Instead the passage was emphasizing the need to look into the message provided by the teachers of the day in order to determine whether they understood a Gospel according to Jesus. However when the gospel according to man is in play it tends to collect its own form of spiritual validation. Thus we also need a way to test the spiritual realm that backs up any message or doctrine. Colossians confirms the victory we have over counterfeit powers.

Colossians 2:15 And having disarmed the powers and authorities, he (Jesus) made a public spectacle of them, triumphing over them by the cross.

So every religious stronghold is a combination of both human desire and spiritual support. On both accounts we should begin to let Jesus challenge the message we have heard and rid us of any demon that has brought us inspiration and validation.

God based on what you did on the Cross, test where I am owned or have been improperly effected by this person's ministry or doctrine, also judge by the Cross any spiritual power that seeks to own me through their teaching.

Cause and effect

I just briefly touched on this subject in a previous chapter, but due to the combination of improper doctrine and spiritual validation, a demonic realm can be given control over our lives. For this reason when we get set free of counterfeit works it is not uncommon to "feel" insecure when a void has been created by a departing power. Since pseudo religious experiences base much of their success on how good we feel, the loss of that feeling needs rectifying. Notice I didn't say "replace one feeling with another": though God is able to refresh us and offer us assurances that go deep within the heart and mind, there are no guarantees that He will support us with something we can measure with our senses. For example, you may have heard the term "the peace that passes all understanding"?

Philippians 4:7And the peace of God, which transcends all understanding, will guard your hearts and your minds in Christ Jesus.

Why don't we understand it? Because it is not acquired through our physical senses. The Spirit of God is not touching our flesh but rather introducing us to His spiritual support. This is also where we find satisfaction and exchange with the God Head. The Father, Son and Holy Spirit are not void of their own emotional make up.

So if we happen to be comforted by the love of God (His attribute) we are not receiving that love thru the vehicle of our flesh but rather with our renewed spirit.

By letting Jesus challenge our doctrinal and spiritual foundations He once again becomes the only source of Christian expression that we need or want. For this reason the one true Savior is never offended in the slightest if we test any point of doctrine or spirit that seeks to portray itself as a messenger of light. The Amplified Version in 1 John 1:4 expounds upon what this test looks like. To "test" is the same as our right to "examine, prove, scrutinize, approve, deem worthy" any perceived influence claiming to be God or of Him.

Application

Jesus,
I recognize that I died with You to the following;
- **To inappropriately basing my deliverance, renewal and future Christian walk on feelings.**
- **To my ability or inability to know when feelings come from You.**
- **To being subject to a spiritual realm and false gods that support inappropriate feelings in my body, soul and spirit.**
- **To exalting myself and inviting seductive spiritual powers to validate my religious choices.**
- **I also died with you to being subject to any spiritual realm that has empowered these issues.**

By virtue of my death, these improper covenants are broken.
I ask You to be the resurrection power that now saves me.

Just on a side note; I realize, from experience, it's not always an easy decision to let go of the counterfeit. Knowing that we may have to say good-bye to a euphoric spiritual encounter often tears at our soul. However a real relationship with the true living God is of greater importance; even if it means we never get to feel that way again. God does support a miraculous life, but how will we know what is truly of Him unless we trust the Cross to purge our previous misconceptions?

The Word without the Spirit

We just talked about the effects of poor doctrine and spiritual involvement that arises through man's opinions and misdirected zeal. However even the scriptures that we read can be misinterpreted when combined with religious motives.

The Word rightly speaks to us regarding the need to put on Christ and shed the nature of fallen Adam. It offers us counsel that comes from the heart of God and lets us explore the nature and character of Jesus. As we grow in relationship with Him the Holy Spirit offers us a constant river of life that does not disappoint. The message remains clear, harmonious and reveals the intent of God's will and purposes.

What we are looking for is a foundation which is based on a combination of God's Spirit and His truth. Together these two components produce "revelation"; in other words "eureka moments" that bring us into proper understanding and practice. They also describe for us the meaning of "sound doctrine". Sound doctrine is not about words on a page, but rather a balance of Spirit and Truth which grants to us access to God's power in both life and in faith.

Now obtaining Spirit and Truth is often easier said then done. Since the majority of believers have a past history of serving religious interests their take on the Word has been colored. Man's natural and intellectual religious pursuits veil a true message.

1 Corinthians 1:18-20 For the message of the cross is foolishness to those who are perishing, but to us who are being saved it is the power of God. For it is written: "I will destroy the wisdom of the wise; the intelligence of the intelligent I will frustrate." Where is the wise person? Where is the teacher of the law? Where is the philosopher of this age? Has not God made foolish the wisdom of the world?

When the wisdom of the world is allowed to filter scripture we look for an "instruction manual" that can tell us how to act in the flesh, rather than function in the Spirit. This trust in man's reason is a form of idolatry and is an example of "word worship". Jesus makes the distinction between truth and error in the following passage:

John 5:39 You diligently study the Scriptures because you think that by them you possess eternal life. These are the Scriptures that testify about me, yet you refuse to come to me to have life.

Jesus was talking to the religious leaders of His day. These men were once ordained by God to preserve His written Word and instruct His people in godliness. Yet these Old Covenant magistrates had placed too much emphasis on their own ability to be righteous. True, the Old Covenant did encourage man to try, yet it was intended to eventually lead them to a dependency on the Messiah. What the religious leaders didn't understand was righteousness could only be achieved through faith in God's Son. These men were depending on their own strength to bring forth the kingdom and it didn't matter how diligently they had studied the scripture, or preached its content, they ended up persecuting the Living Word.

I have personally been over zealous at times for the same reasons. I have sought to delve into the Word of God with a personal agenda in order to support my own religious views. I have also viewed the Word of God through various Christian factions. My motivation in both realms was the same; to gain the proverbial religious prize rather than actually grow in the knowledge of Christ.

Application
Jesus, I repent for bypassing your righteousness and seeking to establish my own.
I recognize that I died with You;
- **To my attempts at owning Your Word and making it say what I want it to say.**
- **To my attempts to follow Your Word based on how others have tried to make it say what they wanted it to.**
- **To my attempts at perfecting the flesh by following natural reason, natural intellect and other peoples opinions regarding biblical truth instead of relying on the power of Your Spirit for biblical counsel.**
- **To being subject to a spiritual realm associated with each faulty attempt.**

By virtue of my death, these improper covenants are broken.
I ask You to be the resurrection power that now saves me.

As believers if we desire to grow in Christ and avoid religious pitfalls it may help if we look a little more closely at today's church model. When a pulpit and pew mentality is present too much emphasis is placed on leadership's ability to hear God for us, study the Word for us and be our Christian conscience. Once we have chosen a leader to represent us in this manner we begin to identify more with the person than we do with Christ. This was also a recognizable problem in Paul's day:

1 Corinthians 3:3-5-13a For when one says, "I follow Paul," and another, "I follow Apollos," are you not mere human beings? 5 What, after all, is Apollos? And what is Paul? Only servants, through whom you came to believe—as the Lord has assigned to each his task. 13 Is Christ divided?

Within that dysfunctional frame work what is lost is an intimate connection with Jesus, a sense of having personal authority and an access to a life made in His image. Some questions worth asking are as follows;

- Have we set aside our own invitation to know Christ for the sake of playing follow the leader?
- Who or what (family, church, leader, doctrine, organization, bad choice, demon, etc.) have we invited to come between us and God?
- Have we given away our birthright to someone else to hear God's voice, know His will or be the voice that speaks for us?

All of these represent bad contracts that allow improper mediation in our relationship with God. Since we each have the Holy Spirit and the Word of God at our disposal that combination is able to create mature sons and daughters without any added interference. To put this into right perspective, no one should ever stand between us and God.

Application
Jesus, I repent for where I have sought to gain the spiritual experience and intellectual knowledge of men, rather than explore a personal invitation to know you and participate in the fruit of Your divine nature.

Linda's Comments
Being the Church is simply the life of Jesus flowing through His body. As a pastor, I am learning to walk again, just like a baby, but this time in His kingdom, not in mine. Just as salvation was all about Him, a healthy expression of church life needs to be all about Him as well.

I encourage you to take a risk and challenge what you think the Church should look like and your commitments to any religious system that you have helped create. I firmly believe that Jesus is quite capable of being the Head of His Church and we can experience this reality if we will just get out of the way.

CHAPTER 7
The Religion of Me

The small group of believers, that once captivated me, no longer holds me captive. Their influence began to be moved out of the way the day that Jesus showed me the importance of His Cross. Though they had appeared spiritually committed and even passionate in their faith they lacked a foundational component which would have kept them on the straight and narrow. Of course, this isn't an isolated occurrence; without the Cross separating us from our natural inclinations all of us are vulnerable to religious decay. Basically if we have failed to put Jesus first on any occasion then we risk measuring Christianity by faulty standards; standards I might add that create a "Me" centered religion.

We have spent considerable time talking about how outside influences affect the quality of our faith. They often press us to move to the beat of a religious drum. Yet our bowing to these added gymnastics really stems from our own fleshly attempts to remain in charge. No one is actually forcing us to submit to their ways or even demanding that we yield to their will; we choose whom we want to serve. So religion has a tendency to rule over us only because we want it to. Yet this "me" centered thinking promotes conclusions that are simply contrary to the life of Christ.

- In our religion we depend on our flesh in order to make Godly choices.
- In our religion we think we are the sum total of all our good and evil experiences.
- In our religion we think Jesus accepts us just the way we are.
- In our religion we define our actions as right or righteous and then defend them as if God agrees with us.
- In our religion personal change comes about only as more rules and stronger forces subdue us.
- In our religion we allow Adamic authority to improperly make spiritual choices for us.
- In our religion it becomes more important to uphold Adamic authority than to trust Christ for answers.

- In our religion there is never equality.
- In our religion we draw from whatever spiritual power will support and validate our choices.
- In our religion we look for a minister and church that can compliment our humanity instead of our newness in Christ.
- In our religion we view others based on who they were rather than who they are in Christ.

These are just a few of the byproducts of a "me" centered religion. I am sure you could think of many more. A faith that is "all about me (or us)" is bound to miss out on the singleness of God's mind and heart. To put this into perspective; ever hear the saying" God is my co-pilot"? If that's the case then you have been sitting in the wrong seat all along!

<u>Application</u>
Jesus, I repent of trying to pursue you in my own strength.
I recognize that I died with You:
- **To defining my Christian walk as if it represents my journey rather than an extension of yours.**
- **To my physical, intellectual, emotional and spiritual attempts to start my own religion.**
- **To my religious attempts to improperly submit to various denominations and authority figures. (Name some)**
- **To my religious attempts at adding doctrines to my faith that have nothing to do with You.**
- **To being subject to the fallen spiritual realm associated with my "me" religion.**

By virtue of my death, these improper covenants are broken.
I ask You to be the resurrection power that now saves me.

So in Christ we have a sure foundation, yet if we have missed a death, burial and resurrection Gospel then we are likely experiencing a self inflicted form of religious bondage. In light of this I believe we can all benefit by going back and reevaluating our understanding of Christian identity.

Our Place in the Kingdom

When we first got saved we were made new and complete; Paul went so far as to say that if <u>any</u> man be in Christ he is a new creation. That new reality includes a number of incredible personal advantages that are laid out in the Word.

John 1:12	I am a child of God.
John 15:15	I am a friend of Jesus.
John 15:16	I'm appointed to bear fruit
Romans 5:9	I have been justified.
Romans 8:1	I am free from condemnation
1Corinthians 3:16	I am the temple of God
1 Corinthians 6:17	I am one with His Spirit.
1 Corinthians 6:19	I belong to God
1 Corinthians 12:27	I am part of Christ's Body
2Corinthians 1:21	I am sealed by God
2 Corinthians 5:17	I am a minister of reconciliation
Ephesians 2:10	I am God's workmanship
Philippians 4:13	I can do all things through Christ
Colossians 1:13	I have been redeemed
Colossians 2:9	I am complete in Christ
Colossians 3:1	I am hidden with Christ in God
2Timmothy 1:7	I have power, love and a sound mind.
Heb. 4:14, Eph. 3:12	I have access to God's throne
1John 5:18	I am born of God and the evil one can not touch me.

These are current truths that define us in Christ and they came about the day we accepted Jesus; they represent a personal position and authority that can never be rescinded. However there is something disquieting about this list. Whenever we participate in religious endeavors we will see the message through a fleshly veil. If you noticed the "I am" and the "I have" references describing each verse then you have spotted the problem. We often view Christianity as if we own it. This is something we convey by saying it is "My Christianity or my salvation". However realistically if I take ownership of that which belongs to God then I risk losing out on a proper relationship and connection with Him. Secondly, it means I will start deciding for myself what should be added and what should be taken away from a true faith. Hence I will often sacrifice truth in Christ in order to support my perceptions of "right"; I decide right doctrine, right spiritual experiences, right morality and right identity. Furthermore I will tend to approach God with the same amount of arrogance. Under such a delusion I will try to convince Him how life and faith should actually work, believing that with time He will eventually come to see things my way. In fact I'm betting on Him changing before I ever do!

As silly as that sounds we all in one way or another want to order life and godliness around what we think is best. This mindset is a part of the god complex that was first presented to Adam and Eve in the garden; "For God knows in the day you eat of the Tree of the knowledge of good and evil you will be like Him knowing good and evil." However life in Christ is not a path that ever glorifies our old man. If we have a mindset that we can do it for God then we suffer under the banner of our own religion. But what does Jesus have to say on the subject?

John 15:5 "I am the vine; you are the branches. If you remain in me and I in you, you will bear much fruit; apart from me you can do nothing.

By choosing to believe Jesus before we trust in ourselves it allows God to be the one that opens up the kingdom for us. We start to see with His eyes and make choices based on His heart. Under such conditions humility brings us the best of what Jesus has to offer. Notice the change in perspective in the following renovated prayer.

Application
Jesus, I recognize that I died with You to embracing these scriptural truths through my own natural man's physical, intellectual, emotional and spiritual logic or prowess. I now agree that my death, burial and resurrection were accomplished by You and I had nothing to do with it.
- **You have made me a child of God. John 1:12**
- **You have made me Your friend. John 15:15**
- **You have appointed me to bear fruit for God. John 15:16**
- **You have justified me. Romans 5:1**
- **You have freed me from condemnation. Romans 8:1**
- **You have made me the temple of God. 1Corinthians 3:16**
- **You have made me one with Your Spirit. 1Corinthians 6:17**
- **You have given me belonging. 1Corinthians 6:19**
- **You have made me part of Your Body. 1Corinthians 12:27**
- **You have sealed me in the Holy Spirit. 2Corinthians 1:21**
- **You have qualified me as a minister of reconciliation. 2Corinthians 5:17**
- **You have made me a new creation. Ephesians 2:10**

- You have empowered me to do all things through You. Philippians 4:13
- You have brought me into redemption. Colossians 1:13
- You have made me complete in You. Colossians 2:9
- You have hidden me in God. Colossians 3:1
- You have provided me a spirit of power, love and a sound mind. 2Timothy 1:7
- You have given me free access to the throne of God. Heb.4:14, Eph.3:12
- You have caused me to be born of God, and have removed me from the evil one's reach. 1John 5:18

By virtue of my death, my improper naturally minded religious roles and expectations are broken.
I now ask You to be the resurrection power that now saves me.

In the days ahead you may become more aware as to how valuable these many promises are now that you have gained access to them through Christ alone. If there is any benefit it will manifest with a solid sense of belonging to Him, His family and His plans regarding salvation and Christianity. This transformed view will also help move you to take personal responsibility for your faith while at the same time find contentment in not "taking over". The Holy Spirit will also likely be able to stir in you a renewed desire to please God and remain more sensitive to His gentle leading. As we trust Him we can be assured that He will begin to show us where bad religion still stands in the way of a complete faith; or better said where we stand in the way of a complete faith.

Spiritually Equipped or Religiously Whipped

When religious principles are at work in our lives they are there because we asked for them and everything we have added to a simple faith is the result of us wanting to be "right" according to our own religious standards. Yet, the connection we are supposed to have with Jesus is internal; He dwells within our hearts and sets in motion a transformation that changes a person from the inside out. However if we define our religion based on external promptings we will likely find ourselves looking good on the outside, but remaining forever deficient on the inside. Let me give you an example of where I once went astray.

There was a time that I was so mesmerized by a leader's ministry style that I set aside my own personal relationship with Jesus just to follow his. I distinctly remember praying and asking God whether I should join this group of believers, but I was so enthralled with their show of piety and power that I didn't actually wait for God's answer. In my natural reasoning I choose a man to lead me based on attributes that were familiar to me. In other words, he reminded me of past authority figures, Christian success stories, past religious interests and traits present in my own family members. For all intents and purposes the man shined with Christian brilliance and he would make a fine addition to my religion. What I had failed to see was that even if the man was a hundred percent right I was choosing to allow someone to stand between me and God. In essence I was choosing a man's religion and ultimately bondage made in his image.

Now there are currently in excess of 40,000 denominations calling themselves "Christian" but only one God. Where did they all come from? Single individuals did the same thing I did; they set aside their own relationship with God in order to trust in some other example of faith.

As Jesus leads you to ponder many of the teachings and spiritual experiences of your past consider taking your denominational issues to the Cross as well. In fact do consider that many of your current troubles, confusion and inconsistencies in the faith may be based on having settled for a second best religion. This can include any participation in the organizational Church, the home group movement or in an improper pursuit of an individual's beliefs.

On that note I created a list of denominations that I once added as a filter on my own understanding of Christianity. Here is my list; Baptists, Presbyterians, Catholics, Assemblies of God, a Bible Church, a community Church, Church of God, a fellowship group, and a Bible College. If you are so inclined I recommend that you create your own list for future reference as well. Here is an example of how I dealt with my list:

Application
Jesus, I recognize that I died with You;
- **To choosing various denominations to be apart of my new religion.**
- **To being subject to my list of religious and denominational ties where I let them improperly subdue or take away my authority in Christ.**
- **To being subject to doctrines, kingdom principles, church, worship, church service, church gifting, and church authority which is veiled by man's religion.**

- To improperly accepting the Baptists, Presbyterians, Catholics, Assemblies of God, a Bible Church, a Community Church, Church of God, a fellowship group, and a Bible College as my new religion.
- To being subject to any spiritual demonic realm that served each of these religious associations.

By virtue of my death, these improper covenants are broken.
I ask You to be the resurrection power that now saves me.

One more point of concern; it is possible to get a distorted view of God Himself from these same past religious associations. If we are willing to test how a religious faction has been allowed to own our walk then we will eventually need to ask "do we have the right god?" Remember the verse in 2 Corinthians 11:3-4 that spoke of another jesus, a different spirit, a different gospel? Well this is where it applies.

Then again if we ever needed a reason to question whether an institutional god was genuine then maybe it is as simple as realizing that God is not a Baptist, a Presbyterian or a Catholic.

Application
Jesus, I recognize that I died with You
- To being subject to any false god that may have supported the work of the (insert you own list, this was mine.) the Baptists, Presbyterians, Catholics, Assemblies of God, a Bible Church, a Community Church, Church of God, a fellowship group, and a Bible College.
- To being subject to any demonic power that interacted with me in the form of a false father God, false Jesus and false Holy spirit.

By virtue of my death, these improper covenants are broken.
I ask You to be the resurrection power that now saves me.
As I have been set free, so has my house been set free.

Dealing with a Push and Pull Religion

When we are in charge of our own religion we depend upon our own strength and discernment in order to succeed. Specifically we set goals for ourselves and then lay hold of concepts which demand religious performance in order to feel complete. However just as abruptly we may also want to pull away from that religion when its demands become to heavy a burden or it simply takes a bite out of us. This push and pull type of motivation is common to all men; its how the flesh deals with life in general. Yet when we got saved we were offered an alternative means for gaining the kingdom and a way to set at bay our past choices. This is where death, burial and resurrection offer us a reprieve.

Tree thinking, if you recall, is all about a balancing act between good and evil. More to the point it's about two responses in life which we are constantly trying to uphold. So we have forward motion and we have reverse, but every attempt at playing the religious game with men, organizations, or a warm fuzzy spiritual realm becomes work for us rather than rest in Christ.

Can we rest now that we are in Jesus?

The answer is yes! If the Cross is at work in our lives then it is able to deal with any subject that makes us push and pull. Here is a way to determine whether there are still some push and pull games present in your own walk with God.

If you have suffered at the hands of people, an organization or a religion then they have likely left an indelible mark on you. So when their name comes up in conversation or when something reminds you of them, do you have an emotional reaction? That reaction is the result of previous preprogramming that either wants to reengage them based on past likes or it can just as easily be a desire to run away from them for what you don't like. But in either case it's a confirmation that you are not actually free from their continued influence. If they still occupy your time and attention you are probably still owned by them and their agendas. The result is a "push and pull" type of bondage that stays with you until you give both responses up to God.

Application

Jesus, I recognize that I died with You;
- **To having a personal religion that draws men, organizations, denominations, a demonic realm or an angelic order near or tries to push them away.**
- **To moving towards a person, organization or religion (Name one) and conditioning my body, soul and spirit to comply.**
- **To also moving away or running away from that person, organization or religion and conditioning my body, soul and spirit to comply.**
- **To also being subject to their improper ownership of me in body, soul and spirit, mind, will, emotions, moral**

conscience, conscious and subconscious thought, intimacy, sexuality, authority, identity, Christianity, family, communication, intellect, and gender, whether I'm coming or going.
- **To being subject to a spiritual realm that supports both the push and the pull of my relationship with them.**

By virtue of my death, these improper covenants are broken.
I ask You to be the resurrection power that now saves me.

On a side note this also works well in bringing separation from sinful behavior. Certainly we are quick to repent to God for our sinful actions but what also needs to be considered is how we once programmed our will to move towards that sin and then also sought to pull away from it. Let Jesus deal with your push and pull struggle with sin.

Application
Jesus, I recognize that I died with You;
- **To moving towards a particular sin (name one) by my own strength.**
- **To moving away from that same sin by my own strength.**
- **To being subject to a spiritual realm and false gods that support both my attempts.**

By virtue of my death, these improper covenants are broken.
I ask You to be the resurrection power that now saves me.

Taking Thoughts Captive

Now initially we don't need God to tell us that we have made some pretty bad choices. If you have suffered defeat in any of your attempts to find Him then you'll know what I mean. I have done some really stupid things in pursuit of God. Such choices affected the direction of my heart and mind putting a damper on my future.

When we take notice of a reoccurring physical, intellectual, emotional or spiritual pattern in our lives it should lead us to ask where and when such behavior first appeared. We can usually track most of our trouble to a first encounter with a person, a group, an organization, or an event. Once we choose to come under or submit to any questionable influence our lives, our goals and our faith get altered. However the Christian is not supposed to be "under" anything since God has seated us in heavenly realms.

Let me offer an example of how I had to make changes in my own life regarding this subject:

> Growing up as the youngest of five kids meant that I often found it easier to go along with the flow. So as brother and sisters impressed upon me the need to conform to their will I often complied. As I grew and left home this learned pattern of submission offered me some advantages in life, but over time it also left me frustrated in my ability to prosper. I had created a pattern of submission that never let me be myself or grow beyond someone else's expectations of me. Yet years later, as I gave thought to how this pattern of unhealthy relational bonds came about all of a sudden I knew that the "root" had to do with my earlier choice to submit. I realized that this behavior problem had been with me for a very long time and as an adult I was still suffering under the power of an adolescent choice. So I took this bad contract of submission to the Cross in order to allow Jesus to set proper boundaries for me within my family as well as within the family of man.

<u>Application</u>
Jesus, I recognize that I died with You;
- **To my young attempts at improperly conforming to will and the wishes of my brother and sisters.**
- **To accepting their improper ownership of me in body, soul and spirit.**
- **To adopting patterns of thought and action that resemble their good and evil ways.**
- **To being subject to a spiritual realm and false gods that support their interests.**

By virtue of my death, these improper covenants are broken.
I ask You to be the resurrection power that now saves me and establishes proper boundaries in my relationships, first with family and then with the rest of the world.

Becoming Aware of Religious Ownership

Our early religious choices deserve just as much attention as our personal issues. In retrospect if we have conformed to the wishes of any religious family we have also given away our authority to them and their gods. Sorry to say even a Dad or Mom's religious history should be set aside in order to receive for ourselves the gift of salvation and relationship with God.

Do all "religious" people and events improperly affect us?
No, not at all; yet when we seek to find our identity in men (generic) rather than in Christ, that is the moment that we are choosing to be under a religious master.

<u>Application</u>
Jesus, I recognize that I died with You;
- To my choices to be subject to prior religious training and subservience.
- To early choices to be made in the image of (Insert your own list of denominations, groups, or individuals) when they fell short of You in Spirit and in Truth.
- To my choices to be made in the image of my Dad's, Mom's, brother's and sister's religion when they fell short of You in Spirit and in Truth.
- To conforming to the image of counterfeit leadership, both domestic and ecumenical, for how I perform in my body, soul and spirit, mind, will, emotions, moral conscience, conscious and subconscious thought, intimacy, sexuality, authority, identity, Christianity, family, communication, intellect, and gender.
- To being subject to a spiritual demonic realm based on the same error in judgment.

By virtue of my death, these improper covenants are broken.
I ask You to be the resurrection power that now saves me.

By taking these patterns of wrong submission to the Cross we are then able to regain the singularity of having Christ's mind and heart. Our actions and behaviors are then more readily able to reflect His nature and character rather than settling for a second best religion. For this reason our personal transformation in Christ may tend to cause a collateral effect.

Relational Responses to Change

As we are experiencing transformation in Christ we should also be aware that relationships are going to go through a certain amount of renovation. You see at one time we were in agreement with others regarding religion. That meant we where united with them in certain practices and rituals. Yet as Jesus has been allowed to bring change to our lives the cords of improper unity have begun to unwind. Please don't misunderstand; we still retain fellowship in Christ when Jesus remains at the foundation; however it's the traditions of men that remain fleeting. Of course the question that is before us is, "How much of our unity was founded upon Christ in the first place and how much of it was based on man's ideals?" The answer will likely decide how strong the cords of faith and friendship really go.

As others begin to see and sense the changes in your life there is some cause and effect dynamics that may arise.

The most favored reaction comes about when a friend or acquaintance comes to understand the same revelation of the Cross and they are just as excited about change as you are. In this instance we each find issues in life where we can shed the old man and gain more of Christ.

Linda and I have had this type of fellowship and we have very much enjoyed the journey. But I must add, there are times that we have had to challenge issues of false fellowship. We have needed to come together in order to talk about what has recently changed in my life or in hers. As we share with one another what God is doing and how He is uprooting strongholds, we are able to resolve relational imbalances when both of us are willing to give the matter to God.

Relationships that are not necessarily based on close friendship will also experience change. However these exchanges may take a different turn.

When human bonds get readjusted people tend to react in fleshly ways. Some will want to try to regain lost ground, and may be frustrated in not knowing how to recapture the past. They may possibly react with hurt feelings, angry responses and even accusatory words. Others may respond with charm, kindness or even flattery in their attempt to regain a lost connection.

There is also a spiritual element being removed from the equation. When we have been divested of improper doctrine and ritual the spiritual support that once accompanied our choices also gets severed. So when unity in a spiritual power is lost others will feel it. Now a demon can't interrupt God's hand of deliverance upon our lives, but they can have a say in the lives of those that are still under their influence. It is not unusual for people to feel as if they have been betrayed or personally rejected when it is simply a loss of improper spiritual connection. A common response then comes into play; they will want to push back with their own attempts at rejection and betrayal. Scripture shows us how to deal with these difficult relational times.

Colossians 3:12-14 Therefore, as God's chosen people, holy and dearly loved, clothe yourselves with compassion, kindness, humility, gentleness and patience. Bear with each other and forgive whatever grievances you may have against one another. Forgive as the Lord forgave you. And over all these virtues put on love, which binds them all together in perfect unity.

If at all possible be at peace with all men, but also realize that in many cases setting aside religious interest means we will no longer have the same motivation, goals or beliefs that we once shared.

Now I would love to save all my past relationships by offering them the message of the Cross; however I know more than ever that I can only plant seeds and must let God provide the right season for their growth. Showing them the love of Christ and sharing how Jesus has transformed my life has relieved some of the tension but ultimately it has been important to let Jesus be their savior in these times of transition. What this means for you and I is that we continue to move forward in God, even if we seem to lose a few connections and friendships along the way.

Forgiveness

Finally when we take responsibility for our walk with God, it will become evident that we have relied too heavily on other people to supply the answers. These people might have been wonderful and upright saints; people that possess a true call upon their lives, yet like all humans, error can interrupt a good thing.

In my own case, prior to understanding the Cross, I didn't know how to correctly separate from the effects of religious people. My response was then to simply put up with questionable practices and follow along in the hopes that something would change for the better. However submission to these people and moments of religious confusion created even greater bondage. The answer was to quit playing the game all together.

As I got free of many of these improper religious bonds at the Cross I initially found myself feeling anger for having been abused by religious people. Yet in those same moments of frustration I came to realize that I needed to forgive them for wherever their humanity interrupted my faith. It didn't matter how we got to this place of contention, what was required was my willingness to move foreword with God in the here and now.

Speaking of God; anger towards religious enterprises may include the belief that God was either present or affirming of the abuse or He was at least not available to save you from trouble. These thoughts are not accurate for sure; God did not create the problem, but rather freewill did. However because mankind is quick to shake his fist at God for any and all reasons, I suggest taking a look inside to determine whether you harbor bitterness towards Him.

Here's the reason we need to forgive; if we feed "unforgiveness" on any level, we continue to allow an offending party to own us in our Christian walk. We also stifle God's ability to move us into His greatest measure of peace and rest. Forgiving is actually one of the simplest and most powerful forms of deliverance we can know.

On a similar note; if you have "served" while under the veil of religious error then it may also be necessary for you to seek forgiveness from others. In light of this a little repentance goes a long way toward healing torn relationships; "I'm sorry, I was wrong," can produce remarkable results and heal friendships.

And finally there is one more action that applies. If in your "Me" centered religion you find yourself devastated by the choices you have made, then you may have to forgive yourself.

I can attest to feeling terribly defeated at some of the choices I made while in service to religion, when all I really wanted was to know God. I guess the best way to describe it is that a veil of shame followed me from that day forward and I needed forgiveness in order to move past a dark period in my Christianity.

Many of the problems we have amassed are because we have created a system of belief that may look good on the surface but is still full of error. So if we are smart enough to let go and let God we will see Him properly clear away the confusion caused by our many religious notions. Whatever the scenario let repentance and forgiveness refocus our attention back on Jesus.

<u>Application</u>
Jesus,
> **I repent for where I have not forgiven others for my hurts.**
> **I repent for not asking for forgiveness when I hurt others.**
> **I repent for not forgiving myself for the mess I have made.**

Lord help me forgive I need you to be the power of forgiveness in me for the following reasons;
- I forgive those that have hurt me in my religious pursuits. (name them) by teaching me a form of godliness that fell short of You in Spirit and in Truth.
- I forgive them for how they have owned and dominated me in body, soul, spirit, mind (conscious and subconscious thought), will, emotions, moral conscience, sexuality, intimacy, authority, identity, Christianity, family, marriage, communication, business, finance, intellect, and gender; even though I was the one asking to be owned by their religion.
- I forgive myself for taking a wrong turn in religion. I forgive myself for bringing shame upon myself and Christianity.
- Jesus forgive me for my actions and my failed attempts at ministering to Your people.

Linda's Comments

As I have come to understand that I died with Christ I have delighted in the fact that the Cross has separated us from this fallen world, the sin nature and any connection to the devil or unclean spirits. But another thing that our death separated us from is our list of grievances, grudges and accusations. When we participate in unforgiveness it pulls us out of the safety of our position in Christ and puts us right back into the strife, contention and darkness of this fallen world. The only thing that holds us in that terrible place is that we have a tight fisted, white knuckled grasp on our offense. As we come to understand the work of the Cross we need to ask ourselves the question, "What can dead people hold on to?" The answer is "nothing". When we truly believe that we have died with Jesus we begin to realize that our hurts, our pain and even our demands for justice died too. In the New Creation He alone is judge and we depend totally upon Him to make things right. Remember, if we are dead we can't hold on. My advice is to accept the reality of your death with Christ and just let go.

CHAPTER 8
The Rest of God

Since God has given us a viable means of clearing the slate, and a wonderful opportunity to move natural and spiritual obstructions out of our way, I guess the next question is, "where do we go from here?"

I'm convinced that most every aspect of life and faith can be transformed in Christ. If you have found any freedom at the Cross then continue to talk to Jesus about change. Be willing to take your thoughts captive and ask questions such as: who and what owns me, where am I still in charge, and where have I given my authority away? God is faithful and will show you the things that stand in the way of relationship with Him.

One of the first and most profound things I began to notice when I took issues to the Cross was I could truly rest in God for the first time in my life. Linda could attest to the fact that when we first met I was pretty high strung. I had taken upon myself the burden of serving religious interests and obligations which eventually went to the extreme. But over time as I laid down many of these religious commitments (contracts), as well as my own attempts at finding God, I started to mellow out quite substantially. Here's just one example of that growing sense of contentment:

One day Linda and I were having a conversation and I had to confess to her that I was struggling with something inside, something I had never experienced before had laid a hold of me and it didn't seem to be diminishing. I felt very strange and it was affecting my whole countenance. I then told her, if I had to guess what this was "I think its peace!"

Rest also encourages us to count our blessings. More specifically when a person enters relationship with Jesus they don't have to keep looking for that connection. Now that may sound a little redundant, except those that are still looking for God are failing to take advantage of that which is already theirs in Christ. This can loosely be compared to any type of relationship; we either have it or we don't. However in Jesus we are talking about a true place of union and an unlimited opportunity to rest in an eternal Person. He remains complete and so does His provision; so look no further. From this day forward we no longer have to work, sacrifice, buy, sell, make vows, plead, or try to manipulate God for the things that are already ours in Him. The nature and character of God, His many attributes, His remarkable anointing, His gifts and even His love have not come about based on working our way to heaven.

If by chance you have ever been caught up in religious antics then you know that within those systems of belief the opposite is true. In religion, most every agenda demands that we follow a dangling carrot; "someday you'll have it, but not today". Sadly even our worship epitomizes a longing, a hunger, and some form of pronouncement that we are dry, dusty and in need of refreshing. As I have discovered even our concepts of "purpose in the Kingdom" need a redeeming breath from God. I remember one such event that was very significant in helping me shed a lot of my religiosity:

> I had believed for years that God was leading me to serve His people in the midst of uncertain times and I was looking forward to investing myself in that endeavor. I felt that God had made it clear that on a particular date I would begin a journey that would catapult me into ministry. I queried about this for a while, but then decided to proceed in faith with a positive outlook. Though many times previously there had been set backs and delays, He assured me that if He didn't come through this time then I was released to go follow my own dreams.
>
> As the date finally arrived, the anticipation left me perched on the edge of my seat. However to my regret I watched as the whole day passed by without any clear answer from God! Another day went by and then a week and then after about ten days, I finally heard the Spirit of God say; "OK you are free to go! I didn't come through on my end, so the deal is off and you are free to go and pursue your own personal dreams and visions. I assure you that I will bless you in anything that you decide to do."
>
> Well, I was happy that I finally got a response from God and at the same time quite disappointed. How could I now stop hoping in this dream that had been a part of my life for so long? I had worked so diligently and it now seemed to be slipping right through my fingers.
>
> After some hesitation, I decided to approach God and ask Him for some clarity; "You mean that there was never a position within ministry for this specific need?" He said "Oh yes, there is an opportunity to serve my people and the call is genuine. However you are now released to do whatever you want to do;

go and enjoy your life and be blessed."

It soon became clear to me that God was saying something that I needed to hear. He was giving me the freedom of having a choice without carrying the burden of having a duty. All of a sudden the Christian life was placed into perspective; all these years I saw the call of God as if it was a job description rather than an extension of a relationship. He was saying that I no longer had to work to gain position, favor or even friendship.

With a smile on my face I said to Him, "it would be my greatest honor to serve my Friend in whatever capacity He has prepared for me!" In that moment a peace settled in my heart and I stopped working "for" God and started to work "with" Him!

Now there is another side to this story that was just as liberating. Jesus had not only freed me from a burden of dutiful service, but God Himself was off the hook. You see if our perceptions of Christian success demand a return on our invested time and materials then somebody had better pay up. If the foundation is based on works then we expect God to work just as hard as we do.

Of course my religious demands upon God were really skewed and it was at this point that I said to Him; God, you are no longer obligated to uphold my expectations. I will no longer demand that you prove yourself to me as savior, healer, or deliverer. You don't even have to answer my soulish prayers.

I didn't hear God speak that day, but I hear Him now;

"I'm still here as your Savior------I'm still here as your Healer------I'm still here as your friend!"

Trusting in God lets us lose our obligation to be "in charge" and also allows us to rest in "His charge". In other words we simply find opportunity to wait upon Jesus for the true meaning of both life and godliness. So;

Let go of your ledger, friend!

Taking Time to Heal

Isaiah 30:15a This is what the Sovereign Lord, the Holy One of Israel, says: "In repentance and rest is your salvation, in quietness and trust is your strength...

As I began to trust Jesus at the Cross I also realized that line upon line of truth was systematically being added to my life, but this time I was gaining understanding of the Christian life based on the

Holy Spirit's leading. A true standard of faith and encouragement was being added and Jesus was now bringing everything into perspective based on His own schedule. For this reason I have not been in a hurry to rebuild my understanding of church life or act in a hasty manner to defend old beliefs. I find myself waiting for the Spirit of God to direct me daily.

Another benefit of rest is that it is easier to hear God's voice and capture the essence of His heart. Since human nature often relies upon our senses to be the barometer for determining right living, it is also our senses that get used to the religious noise. The noise that we speak of is the anxiety and strife that comes from feeling obligated to do for God rather than simply being with Him. So as the proverbial chatter gets louder with every move towards busyness we miss out on an invitation that leads us beside still waters. One Old Testament story that provides insights into God's quiet side can be seen in a story about Elijah.

1 Kings 19:11-13 The Lord said (to Elijah), "Go out and stand on the mountain in the presence of the Lord, for the Lord is about to pass by." Then a great and powerful wind tore the mountains apart and shattered the rocks before the Lord, but the Lord was not in the wind. After the wind there was an earthquake, but the Lord was not in the earthquake. 12 After the earthquake came a fire, but the Lord was not in the fire. And after the fire came a gentle whisper. 13 When Elijah heard it, he pulled his cloak over his face and went out and stood at the mouth of the cave.

If you have been serving a faith that looks for God in the wind, the quake or the fire then you are now being given a chance to slow down and give up some of your heightened expectations. Let go of your human tenacity in order to wait upon God. Such a quite spirit still leaves room for being inquisitive about the Savior, and offers us His greatest expression of liberty.

Psalm 2:1-3 The Lord is my shepherd, I lack nothing. 2 He makes me lie down in green pastures, he leads me beside quiet waters, 3 he refreshes my soul. He guides me along the right paths for his name's sake.

Finally rest in God also allows us the opportunity to concentrate on Jesus in a one on one capacity. It means that this journey with Him becomes very intimate and personal; it frees us from having to be corporate minded and corporate bound. All too often a new believer is thrust into a church setting where the individual gets lost in a crowd. The consensus has been that there is strength in numbers and that a combined assault on the throne of God will gain His attention. Now we don't deny the Body of Christ their rightful place in our lives, but if the honeymoon period with God was never properly established then there tends to be a trust in men rather than God to bring forth the kingdom. Christianity should be about what God has to say to the individual as well as what the individual has to say back to God. It's a slow dance that lets us ponder what it means to be personally saved and equipped. Only then do we have something to offer the Body of Christ.

In Conclusion

In the days ahead you can expect that the Spirit of God is going to be nudging you to consider many of your previous commitments; many of which have kept you distracted if not exhausted in your pursuit of Him. He will likely call to mind some defining moment, event or exchange that once made you create an "improper" contract with religion. Or it maybe you once submitted to some other type of improper ownership. Notice I said "improper"; not every exchange draws to the surface a bad association or a bad contract, yet who but God can actually decide what is proper and improper about each one? By trusting Him to look into the matter, far beyond the limits of our own reach we are then able to regain a healthy foundation of fellowship, a healthy trust in Christ and an opportunity to be productive saints, all to the glory of God.

Jesus, I can see that it is now day!

Yes, my child,

    It will be day

        for a very long time.

Book 2 Now Available

"The Shadow of the Spiritual" is a meaty, thought provoking, in-depth look into the rising tide of spiritual pollution within the Church. Its lingering effects remain oppressive and damaging to any believer who desires a pure expression of relationship with the Son of God. This self help book is a must read for any Christian wanting to understand how improper spiritual connections get formed, fed and passed around and how God provides a simple solution to rectifying the problem at the Cross.

Another Book on the Way
Book 3

"A Christian guide to biblical deliverance" explains the way in which believers retain freedom in Christ and regain freedom when it's been lost. Because we are often made subject to worldly pressures God has provided us a way of escape which is able to set us free in physical, intellectual, emotional and spiritual ways just for the asking.

Question and Answers

1. Do I have to use the term "I recognize I died"?
No, not at all; you should be free to talk to God in your own way. But it is important to have a solid understanding of what the Cross did on your behalf.

Say it any way you like; "Jesus test by the Cross, take it to the Cross, I died at the Cross, I died and you live etc. etc.

I would also encourage you to every once in a while, return to explaining to God what it means to have passed from death into new life. This time of re-clarification keeps your confession fresh and in tune with God's genuine ministry and power to transform your life.

2. Should I say prayers or declarations out loud?
It's recommended. When you speak out loud on any occasion there is a certain amount of commitment that takes place within the mind and heart. It requires that you speak about the things that are important to you and it requires that you get your thoughts in order. So the same motivation should be used when speaking to God about change for your life.

But let me add one more thought on this subject. Where does God dwell? He dwells in your heart and hears your inner most thoughts. Once you able to speak candidly about what troubles you then an inner conversation with God can be just as effective.

3. Why do I now feel separated from the people and leadership of my church?
When we call upon God to take us to the Cross we are being spiritually transformed by the power of the Holy Spirit. Actions that were once based on our strength get replaced with God's ability to make all things new. Hence fellowship that was once based on human ingenuity doesn't carry the same allure that it once did and we now no longer feel compelled to be a part of the pack.

4. I feel different, is this normal change?
We place a lot of emphasis on our feelings and often measure success by them. However since we have chosen to find transformation in Christ we are letting go of our past barometer in order to find solace in Him. Thus you may need to get accustomed to "peace and rest" being the primary feelings that arise once you resolve an issue before God.

You may also find that deliverance from a previous bad contract does not produce any feeling at all. However the response we are looking for is a changed life; did your words when spoken to Jesus make a positive change in your lifestyle?

5. **I feel undone when I do a declaration; I'm kind of nervous inside, how can you help?**

When you choose to participate in any religious practice you are setting body, soul and spirit into motion, with the intention of pleasing God and men alike. This choice is an act of "your will" and represents a behavior that you adopt while in service. The longer you seek to conform and perform for religion the deeper the entrenchment of certain behaviors go. So when God releases you from improper ownership associated with men, organizations, religion, or a demonic realm ask him to also release you from that learned response or behavior that once accompanied your commitments.

<u>Application</u>
Jesus, as it applies to all the prayers that I have previously declared; I recognize that I died with You to having created a behavior that serves religious men, organizations, denominations, or a demonic power.
By virtue of my death, these improper covenants are broken.
I ask You to be the resurrection power that now saves me.

6. **To be honest I now feel quite depraved in how I have lived the Christian life; is that normal?**

When we serve in religion we are obligated to put our best foot forward at all times. That means we have to prove to others, as well as to ourselves, that we are good enough to play the game. So doing good and being good within the confines of religion offers us a false sense of security. It also denies us the opportunity to open up to God regarding the darkness that is still hiding in our hearts.

However as the religious veil is removed we are then able to compare ourselves to Christ alone. This moment of exposure is not for our destruction but rather for gaining a greater sense of salvation. All of a sudden we know beyond a shadow of a doubt that Jesus is the only one capable of offering us a holy existence and we are glad that He is there with His provision and not condemning us.

Putting this into perspective, religion often judges us without mercy and makes us want to hide our deepest darkest secrets; thus we don't get free of the past. Yet in Christ I can now talk to God (not to men) about the vilest things that I have done, knowing that He is able to set me free of each point of bondage at the Cross.

7. **To be honest I've lost interest and motivation in certain church functions and activities is there something wrong?**

No, just the opposite; you are finally understanding that many of these functions and activities have nothing to do with new life in Christ. I think Linda said it best; "If the Church <u>understood</u> the importance of the Cross a large percentage of what we do in Church practice would be unnecessary and cease to exist."

8. I'm thinking about leaving my Church, is there any where I can go.

First of all let God make that decision for you, but if you feel He is saying its time then consider there may be a season that He asks you to walk alone. It is not that He is denying you fellowship, but rather He may want you to truly come to understand the importance of an intimate relationship with Him first and foremost. If you have never actually been able to mature due to having been kidnapped by religion; then gaining personal time is invaluable to creating a solid anchor in Christ. A time of solace also teaches us to rely upon Him for all things. It also confirms that we have purpose and a place in the kingdom apart from the commission of men.

My advice is to take a few steps back and take time to get to know the Savior. Secondly when you feel it is time ask God to connect you with friends that understand the importance of the Cross in their lives. That may only lead you to fellowship with one or two*, but I believe it is important to let this revelation of the Cross grow organically. I.e. let God make it grow on His time table. Then, as you gain a solid foundation and trust that Jesus is able to complete you; opportunities will emerge for you to meet larger segments of the Church.

The only exception to this advice would be for a pastor that has the podium at their disposal. The pastor has a remarkable opportunity to share the good news with many. As God moves upon leadership to first understand the significance of the Cross, the congregation will prosper.

<u>Application</u>
Jesus, I ask that you will connect me with people that are beginning to understand a revelation of our death, burial, and resurrection with You.

About the Author

Gordon has lived in the Pacific Northwest since his early teens and has a deep love for the beauty of this region. An avid recumbent bicyclist and motorcyclist he can often be seen riding to his favorite table at a riverside park where most of his books have been written. He spent many years in retail management, maintenance supervision and dabbled in invention, but his real love is ministering to the Church.

A believer since early childhood he has served and ministered with devotion in several denominational groups, with a slant towards deliverance ministry. However he came to a crisis of faith in his late thirties that caused him to reevaluate what it means to be genuine before God. Jesus answered that quest with a personal, transforming and powerful understanding of what He had accomplished on the Cross.

Come visit us at Shadow Free Ministries on the World Wide Web

www.shadow-free.com

Shadow Free Ministries offers a web site exploring all the benefits of our death with Christ.

Look for articles and insights leading to a greater awareness of our salvation and deliverance in Jesus.

The most precious of promises can be realized when we come

Out from the Shadow of Other Gods

www.ingramcontent.com/pod-product-compliance
Lightning Source LLC
Chambersburg PA
CBHW071519040426
42444CB00008B/1721